INSTITUTE OF PACIFIC RELATIONS

INQUIRY SERIES

THE INSTITUTE OF PACIFIC RELATIONS

The Institute of Pacific Relations is an unofficial and non-political body, founded in 1925 to facilitate the scientific study of the peoples of the Pacific Area. It is composed of National Councils in eleven countries.

The Institute as such and the National Councils of which it is composed are precluded from expressing an opinion on any aspect of national or international affairs; opinions expressed in this study are, therefore, purely individual.

NATIONAL COUNCILS OF THE INSTITUTE

American Council, Institute of Pacific Relations

Australian Institute of International Affairs

Canadian Institute of International Affairs

China Institute of Pacific Relations

Comité d'Études des Problèmes du Pacifique

Japanese Council, Institute of Pacific Relations

Netherlands-Netherlands Indies Council, Institute of Pacific Relations

New Zealand Institute of International Affairs

Philippine Council, Institute of Pacific Relations

Royal Institute of International Affairs

U.S.S.R. Council, Institute of Pacific Relations

AMERICAN POLICY IN THE FAR EAST: 1931 - 1940

Some Other Studies Already Completed in the I. P. R. Inquiry Series

JAPANESE INDUSTRY: ITS RECENT DEVELOPMENT AND PRESENT CONDITION, *by* G. C. Allen

AUSTRALIA'S INTERESTS AND POLICIES IN THE FAR EAST, *by* Jack Shepherd

GERMAN INTERESTS AND POLICIES IN THE FAR EAST, *by* Kurt Bloch

THE PROBLEM OF JAPANESE TRADE EXPANSION IN THE POST-WAR SITUATION, *by* Miriam S. Farley

NEW ZEALAND'S INTERESTS AND POLICIES IN THE FAR EAST, *by* Ian F. G. Milner

JAPAN'S EMERGENCE AS A MODERN STATE, *by* E. Herbert Norman

THE CHINESE ARMY, *by* Evans Fordyce Carlson

BRITISH RELATIONS WITH CHINA: 1931-1940, *by* Irving S. Friedman

AMERICAN POLICY IN THE FAR EAST

1931 - 1940

By

T. A. BISSON

I. P. R. INQUIRY SERIES

INTERNATIONAL SECRETARIAT
INSTITUTE OF PACIFIC RELATIONS
PUBLICATIONS OFFICE, 129 EAST 52ND STREET, NEW YORK
1940

PRINTED IN THE UNITED STATES OF AMERICA
BY THE HADDON CRAFTSMEN, INC.

FOREWORD

This study forms part of the documentation of an Inquiry organized by the Institute of Pacific Relations into the problems arising from the conflict in the Far East.

It has been prepared by Mr. T. A. Bisson of the Research Staff of the Foreign Policy Association, New York; author of *Japan in China* (1938).

The study has been submitted in draft to a number of authorities including the following, many of whom made suggestions and criticisms which were of great value in the process of revision: Dr. George H. Blakeslee, Professor Denna F. Fleming, and Mr. Jack Shepherd.

Though many of the comments received have been incorporated in the final text, the above authorities do not of course accept responsibility for the study. The statements of fact or of opinion appearing herein do not represent the views of the Institute of Pacific Relations or of the Pacific Council or of any of the National Councils. Such statements are made on the sole responsibility of the author. The Japanese Council has not found it possible to participate in the Inquiry, and assumes, therefore, no responsibility either for its results or for its organization.

During 1938 the Inquiry was carried on under the general direction of Dr. J. W. Dafoe as Chairman of the Pacific Council and in 1939 under his successor Dr. Philip C. Jessup. Every member of the International Secretariat has contributed to the research and editorial work in connection with the Inquiry, but special mention should be made of Mr. W. L. Holland, Miss Kate Mitchell and Miss Hilda Austern, who have carried the major share of this responsibility.

In the general conduct of this Inquiry into the problems arising from the conflict in the Far East the Institute has benefited by the counsel of the following Advisers:

Professor H. F. Angus of the University of British Columbia
Dr. J. B. Condliffe of the University of California
M. Etienne Dennery of the Ecole des Sciences Politiques

These Advisers have co-operated with the Chairman and the Secretary-General in an effort to insure that the publications issued in connection with the Inquiry conform to a proper standard of sound and impartial scholarship. Each manuscript has been submitted to at least two of the Advisers and although they do not necessarily subscribe to the statements or views in this or any of the studies, they consider this study to be a useful contribution to the subject of the Inquiry.

The purpose of this Inquiry is to relate unofficial scholarship to the problems arising from the present situation in the Far East. Its purpose is to provide members of the Institute in all countries and the members of I.P.R. Conferences with an impartial and constructive analysis of the situation in the Far East with a view to indicating the major issues which must be considered in any future adjustment of international relations in that area. To this end, the analysis will include an account of the economic and political conditions which produced the situation existing in July 1937, with respect to China, to Japan and to the other foreign Powers concerned; an evaluation of developments during the war period which appear to indicate important trends in the policies and programs of all the Powers in relation to the Far Eastern situation; and finally, an estimate of the principal political, economic and social conditions which may be expected in a post-war period, the possible forms of adjustment which might be applied under these conditions, and the effects of such adjustments upon the countries concerned.

The Inquiry does not propose to "document" a specific plan for dealing with the Far Eastern situation. Its aim is to focus available information on the present crisis in forms which will be useful to those who lack either the time or the expert knowledge to study the vast amount of material now appearing or already published in a number of languages. Attention may also be drawn to a series of studies on topics bearing on the Far Eastern situation which is being prepared by the Japanese Council. That series is being undertaken entirely independently of this Inquiry, and for its organization and publication the Japanese Council alone is responsible.

The present study, "American Policy in the Far East: 1931-1940," falls within the framework of the first of the four general groups of studies which it is proposed to make as follows:

I. The political and economic conditions which have contributed to the present course of the policies of Western Powers in the Far East; their territorial and economic interests; the effects of their Far Eastern policies, of internal economic and political developments and of developments in their foreign policies vis-a-vis other parts of the world; the probable effects of the present conflict on their positions in the Far East; their changing attitudes and policies with respect to their future relations in that area.

II. The political and economic conditions which have contributed to the present course of Japanese foreign policy and possible important future developments; the extent to which Japan's policy toward China has been influenced by Japan's geographic conditions and material resources, by special features in the political and economic organization of Japan which directly or indirectly affect the formulation of her present foreign policy, by economic and political developments in China, by the external policies of other Powers affecting Japan; the principal political, economic and social factors which may be expected in a post-war Japan; possible and probable adjustments on the part of other nations which could aid in the solution of Japan's fundamental problems.

III. The political and economic conditions which have contributed to the present course of Chinese foreign policy and possible important future developments; Chinese unification and reconstruction, 1931-37, and steps leading toward the policy of united national resistance to Japan; the present degree of political cohesion and economic strength; effects of resistance and current developments on the position of foreign interests in China and changes in China's relations with foreign Powers; the principal political, economic and social factors which may be expected in a post-war China;

possible and probable adjustments on the part of other nations which could aid in the solution of China's fundamental problems.

IV. Possible methods for the adjustment of specific problems, in the light of information and suggestions presented in the three studies outlined above; analysis of previous attempts at bilateral or multilateral adjustments of political and economic relations in the Pacific and causes of their success or failure; types of administrative procedures and controls already tried out and their relative effectiveness; the major issues likely to require international adjustment in a post-war period and the most hopeful methods which might be devised to meet them; necessary adjustments by the Powers concerned; the basic requirements of a practical system of international organization which could promote the security and peaceful development of the countries of the Pacific area.

EDWARD C. CARTER
Secretary-General

New York,
March 12, 1940

CONTENTS

DOCUMENTS

AMERICAN POLICY IN THE FAR EAST:

1931 - 1940

CHAPTER I

INTRODUCTION

In the Far East, no less than in Europe, collapse of the post-war stabilization has assumed steadily increasing momentum since the world depression of 1929-32. The first unmistakable signal heralding this break-down, in fact, was sounded by Japan's military intervention in Manchuria on September 18, 1931. As events progressed, the agreements reached at the Washington Conference—both in the political and naval spheres—were gradually undermined and then swept away. All the basic Far Eastern issues, which are of traditional concern to the United States, have thus been reopened. Beyond the eventual outcome of current Sino-Japanese hostilities, or of any larger conflict which may ensue, lies the comprehensive problem of formulating the bases of a new Far Eastern settlement. It is already apparent that achievement of such new arrangements, on terms which can hold out the promise of greater stability and permanence, will constitute an even more exacting task than that which faced the powers two decades ago. It may be assumed further that the United States, in view of its historic policy and present attitude, is likely to exert an important influence on the ultimate settlement.

The contemporary upheaval in the Far East, both in scope and significance, invites comparison with two previous periods: the threatened break-up of China in 1895-1905, and the World War crisis of 1914-22. There is an underlying similarity in the broad pattern of events during these periods. They correspond to clearly marked phases of imperialist expansion and conflict, in which the driving forces behind the struggle for control of undeveloped areas received sharpest expression. They are linked by the common phenomenon of an aggressive assault on China's national integrity, either by one or more powers. Each time, moreover, the United States has reacted in markedly similar ways. In the first case, during the closing years of the nineteenth century, the principles of American Far Eastern policy were enunciated in their characteristic, present-day form. Up to that time the United States, despite an early and continuous interest in the Far East, had been able to keep the problems of the western Pacific more or less at arm's length. Not until the break-up of China seemed imminent and the Philippine Islands were acquired did the full implications of the American connection with the Far East begin to emerge. Only then did the central issues assume the familiar form which they occupy today in the American public mind.

The policy enunciated by John Hay at this period was a natural outgrowth of traditions and practices developed in the nineteenth century, as well as a response to a narrowing world which intensified the imperialist conflicts revolving about China. The United States had held an important stake in the early Canton trade—a commercial interest which dated from the beginning of its national history. It had been influential in the "opening" of both China and Japan, and it had steadily insisted on the right to a most-favored-nation position. For the American trader in China the watchword was equality of commercial opportunity, and the State Department supported him in this demand. The United States had not sought to obtain territorial holdings in China. At Shanghai and Tientsin, for example, it had not even taken advantage of the opportunity to establish American concessions. On the other hand the United States, like the European powers, had contracted for and enjoyed the special privileges accruing from the "unequal treaties" with China and Japan. American nationals not only shared the advantages of concession areas, but participated directly in the governing body of the Shanghai International Settlement—the most important bit of China's *terra irredenta.* These general characteristics of American policy in the Far East, though not formulated in precise terms, were supported by an accumulated record of diplomatic common law—itself a very substantial sanction.

At the end of the century, several developments of fundamental importance combined to produce a more clear-cut definition of America's role in the western Pacific. Japan's decisive victory over a decadent Manchu Dynasty in 1894-5 occurred at a moment when the European powers were racing to establish their respective claims to the last "free" areas in the world. It stimulated an immediate scramble for leaseholds and other appurtenances of "spheres of interest"—that is, eventual protectorates—in China. The growing possibility of a comprehensive dismemberment and partition of the country raised a threat to equality of commercial opportunity which had not previously been presented in comparable terms. It could be effectively countered by nothing short of a positive reaffirmation, along with active support, of the basic Far Eastern policy of the United States. The pressure for a new American initiative created by conditions in the Far East was reinforced by changes within the United States. For a generation after the Civil War, the task of internal development had largely absorbed the attention of the American people. The disappearance of the frontier heralded the end of this period, and the Spanish-American War ushered in its successor. In an imperialist epoch, the United States had also come of age. Annexation of the Philippine Islands in 1898, coupled with the open door notes of 1899 and 1900, were not accidental phenomena. They inaugurated the contemporary era of American Far Eastern policy. Acquisition of the Philippines, even though it gave the United States an important territorial stake in the Far East for the first time, was auxiliary and incidental. Central emphasis was placed on a declaration: that the United States did not intend to be debarred from participating in the future economic development of eastern Asia. This emphasis has never been outgrown, nor substantially altered. It still holds the field today as the leading directive for American policy in the Far East.

Great Britain collaborated intimately with the United States in formulating and supporting the open door initiatives taken during the 1899-1900 period, when British policy was directed toward winning allies to help check Russian encroachments on China. This fact has sometimes been presented in such a way as to suggest the conclusion that the United States was made the pawn of British diplomacy at the turn of the century.[1] But such a thesis implies that the United States itself was embarking on a new departure in policy, and that this departure was not consonant with American interests. Actually, the effort to assure equality of commercial opportunity in China for the United States and its nationals was characteristic of American policy throughout the nineteenth century. The open door notes merely formulated this principle of American policy in more

[1] For example, A. Whitney Griswold, *The Far Eastern Policy of the United States*. Harcourt, Brace and Company, 1938. Chapter II.

explicit terms. New economic pressures from within the United States, moreover, were developing an even stronger urge at this period toward ensuring participation of American trading and business interests in the development of China. The United States, no less than Britain, had its reasons for working to prevent the threatened "break-up of China." On many occasions since 1899-1900, the two countries have followed a common policy in the Far East; at other times, there has been the sharpest antagonism. Co-operative action, when achieved, need not imply that either party is being made the pawn of the other.

American insistence on the open door principle is not peculiar to China. In the Far East, however, it bears the special characteristic of a concern for China's territorial and administrative integrity. The fulcrum of Far Eastern politics, on which the policies of all powers including the United States have turned, has been the weakness of China. Throughout the present century, China's weakness has continued to be a standing invitation to aggression. An essential element of the open door policy was that sufficient restraint should be placed on aggression to enable China to develop cohesion and strength. The alternative was subjugation by one power or partition by several, in which case equality of commercial opportunity would disappear. For four decades there has been a race between these two contradictory lines of development. China's weakness has proved difficult to overcome. The Manchu Dynasty could not cope with the double task of internal modernization and defense against foreign encroachments. Yuan Shih-kai also failed, and his regime was succeeded by ten years of disorganization and civil war bordering on chaos. Not until the more recent Kuomintang era did signs of progress appear. It is a present-day irony that the most determined assault on China's integrity occurred at a time when China's internal consolidation had achieved its greatest advance.

During these four decades the open door doctrine was but imperfectly maintained. The partial effectiveness which it achieved was due perhaps as much to the conflicting aims of the various powers as to the support of the United States. In everyday practice it preserved for China a nominal independence, while subordinating the country to a semi-colonial status under which all powers could pursue varying degrees of economic and political penetration. China's economic development proceeded on a haphazard basis, mainly along lines desired by the foreign powers. The full-rounded exploitation of China's national resources, which required an independent economic program under Chinese national control, could not take place. At the same time, this partially effective application of the open door principle was extremely significant in one respect. The preservation of a nominal independence gave an opportunity for the forces of Chinese nationalism, germinating slowly in China's old and conservative culture, to assert themselves and establish stability. To this extent, the theoretical sovereignty left to China held within itself the possibility of being transformed into actual sovereignty. And this prospect, in turn, envisaged appearance of the main requisite for a more stable basis for peace in the Far East, that is, a strong and united China capable of protecting its independence by its own efforts. Under such conditions the open door doctrine, in its specifically Chinese application, would become an anachronism and cease to exist.

The methods by which the United States has sought to maintain equality of commercial opportunity in China, as well as its important corollary of China's integrity, have run along opportunistic, trial-and-error channels. They have nowhere been explicitly formulated. Yet certain broad lines of tactical approach during such critical periods as those of 1895-1905, 1914-22, and the present have been well established. Reservation of American rights is always carefully declared, either in diplomatic memoranda or notes of protest. Marked unwillingness to pass beyond this step then gives rise to a negative state of passivity and apparent inaction. Even measures "short of war," if they may be interpreted as at all provocative, are avoided. During this inactive period, efforts within the purely domestic competence of the United States may be made to weight the balance, as by strengthening the navy. Co-operative action with other powers may or may not be sought. If achieved, it is generally held within the same narrow limits, that is, no more active form of coercion than common diplomatic protests. The underlying tendency is to wait until a favorable shift in the balance of power can permit effective diplomatic intervention to restore the *status quo ante*, or as near an approximation of it as possible.

The Open Door Doctrine: First Test

The earliest example of the application of these principles and methods of American policy in the Far East occurred between 1895 and 1905. They could not achieve full, modern expression until this period, when the possibility of China's disappearance as an independent national entity first became actual. Even a cursory survey of events at the turn of the century thus offers valuable indications for the analysis of contemporary American policy.

The cycle between the Sino-Japanese War and the Russo-Japanese War passed through several distinct phases. By the Treaty of Shimonoseki, signed on April 17, 1895, Japan secured Formosa and the Pescadores and recognition by China of Korea's autonomy, but the intervention of Russia, France and Germany forced retrocession of the Liaotung Peninsula. Up to this point the United States had remained on the sidelines. The enforced cession of the Dalny-Port Arthur leasehold to Russia, countered in turn by similar German, British and French moves, however, led to the issuance on September 6, 1899 of John Hay's circular note, requesting assurances from the various powers that equality of commercial opportunity affecting treaty ports, tariffs, harbor dues, and railroad charges would be maintained within their "spheres of interest" in China.[2]

Effective application of this open door principle, which was basically incompatible with further development of the "sphere of interest" conception, required positive support of Chinese sovereignty. The logical extension of the principle was made by Secretary Hay in 1900, when the Boxer Rebellion had created new dangers to China's independence. At this time, in a circular note to American diplomatic representatives, he stated that "the policy of the United States is to seek a solution which may bring about permanent safety and peace to China, preserve Chinese territorial and administrative entity, protect all rights guaranteed to friendly powers by treaty and international law, and safeguard for the world the principle of equal and impartial trade with the Chinese Empire."[3] The Boxer Protocol, concluded by the powers in 1901, levied a crushing indemnity on China and permitted foreign troops to be stationed at certain towns and cities in North China, but contained no territorial cessions. During the negotiations leading to signature of the Protocol, the United States exerted its influence against provisions which would unduly weaken the Chinese government.

[2] *Foreign Relations of the United States, 1899,* pp. 129-30.
[3] *Foreign Relations of the United States, 1900,* p. 299.

Before this settlement was reached, the aggressive policy of Tsarist Russia in Manchuria had become the most immediate threat to China's territorial integrity. During the Boxer Rebellion large numbers of Russian troops had entered Manchuria, and within a short time Russian officers had largely superseded the local Chinese authorities. This Russian military penetration of Manchuria, in conjunction with the fortification of Port Arthur and the newly built railways to Vladivostok and Dalny, bade fair to pass into definitive occupation and eventual annexation. Under these circumstances, the State Department's action was mainly restricted to a series of diplomatic protests, which on the whole, made slight impression on the Tsarist officials.[4] The Russian activities, in Korea even more than Manchuria, also came into conflict with Japan's continental program. Japanese efforts to obtain positive support from the United States in defense of the open door, however, elicited cautious response. In reply to a direct inquiry from Japan regarding American policy, Secretary Hay stated on February 1, 1901 that "we were not at present prepared to attempt singly, or in concert with other Powers, to enforce" our views as to the integrity of China "by any demonstration which could present a character of hostility to any other Power."[5]

During the following year Japan concluded the alliance with Great Britain, and in 1904-5 the Russian advance was halted by Japanese arms. The United States, as well as Great Britain, was generally sympathetic toward Japan's cause in the Russo-Japanese War. Its chief concern, nevertheless, was for the eventual status of Manchuria, and American opinion underwent a remarkable shift after Japan had won the war. President Roosevelt, whose mediation was instrumental in achieving the peace settlement at Portsmouth on September 5, 1905, had sought and obtained prior assurances from Japan respecting Chinese sovereignty in Manchuria. The treaty itself contained a provision binding Japan and Russia "not to obstruct any general measures common to all countries, which China may take for the development of the commerce and industry of Manchuria."[6] Insertion of this clause in the Portsmouth Treaty proved easier

[4] On one occasion during this period the United States sent a naval vessel to Newchwang to support the American consul and the American position.

[5] Quoted by Alfred L. P. Dennis, *Adventures in American Diplomacy, 1896-1906.* New York, E. P. Dutton, 1928. p. 242.

[6] John V. A. MacMurray, *Treaties, etc.,* Vol. I, p. 523.

to obtain than its enforcement, as lengthy diplomatic exchanges with Japan in 1905-6 and the subsequent controversies over American and British railway projects in Manchuria indicated.

Conditions established in Manchuria, in fact, were by no means satisfactory from the American point of view. A Russo-Japanese balance of power tended to pass into Russian and Japanese spheres of influence. In the north, the Chinese Eastern Railway remained under Russian control, while in the south Japan held the Dairen leasehold and the South Manchuria Railway. Subject to these derogations, and to limitations on full equality of commercial opportunity imposed by Japan and Russia, formal Chinese sovereignty was maintained in Manchuria. Its effective assertion depended, in the last analysis, on the degree to which China could develop unity and strength.

Reviewing the whole decade, however, the fact remains that the United States was extraordinarily successful in attaining its general aims during an extremely difficult period. Conversion of the "spheres of interest" into exclusive protectorates, which seemed inevitable for a time, was forestalled. Despite the dangers occasioned by the Boxer Rebellion, no further territories were wrested from China as a consequence of this upheaval.[7] Annexation of Manchuria by either Russia or Japan was prevented, and Chinese sovereignty was formally maintained. These results were achieved by methods which exhibited a caution typical of American Far Eastern Policy.

The World War and Its Aftermath

The Portsmouth Treaty settlement remained effective for nearly a decade, until the outbreak of the World War in August 1914. During this period the Manchu Dynasty was overthrown and a republic proclaimed in China, although the latter passed almost immediately under Yuan Shih-kai's dictatorial control. Important changes also occurred in Japan. At the end of the first Sino-Japanese War, the terms imposed by Japan had established its equality with the Western powers *vis-à-vis* China. So far as status was concerned, the clause of the Shimonoseki Treaty granting Japan most-favored-nation treatment, i.e., extraterritorial and tariff privileges in China, was more noteworthy

[7] In later years, moreover, the United States took the lead in lifting the heaviest imposition of the Protocol by remission of the Boxer Indemnity—an example which was eventually followed by the other powers.

than the territorial and indemnity clauses.[8] After the Russo-Japanese War, the sum total of the territories wrested from China by Japan, including Formosa, the Pescadores and Korea,[9] together with the special position held in South Manchuria, compared not unfavorably with the territories and leaseholds acquired by Great Britain, France or Germany since 1842. Industrialization, fostered at first by direct government support, was gradually transforming Japan's economy. Foreign trade, which totalled only ¥390 millions in 1896, advanced to ¥810 millions in 1905 and to ¥1,362 millions in 1913.[10] In modern industrial technique, however, Japan still lagged behind the advanced Western powers in 1914; the relative success of its territorial expansion was due more to nearness to the scene of action and to possession of a strong military-naval striking force.

These advantages became especially obvious at the outset of the World War, when the Western powers' attention was concentrated on the European battlefields. For Japan the impulse to accept this invitation to continental empire was not weakened by still vivid memories: certain episodes during the "opening" of the country in the mid-nineteenth century; the tripartite intervention of 1895; and the galling weight of extraterritorial and statutory tariff shackles, the latter of which had not been fully removed until 1912. The invitation was accepted with gusto.

Within the brief space of three years, Japan had taken a series of giant strides toward a position of dominance in the Far East. Complete military occupation of the German leasehold at Tsingtao was effected during the autumn months of 1914. Treaties and notes signed with China on May 25, 1915, as a result of the Twenty-One Demands, confirmed Japan in the disposition of all German "rights, interests and concessions" in Shantung province. In addition, they extended the term of Japan's Dairen-Port Arthur leasehold (due to expire in 1923) to 1997, of the South Manchuria Railway to 2002, and of the Antung-Mukden Railway to 2007; granted a number of important economic and political privileges to Japan in South Manchuria and

[8] An anomalous situation, by which Japan enjoyed extraterritorial rights in China while subjected to the disabilities of the system at home, existed from April 17, 1895 to August 4, 1899.

[9] Japan formally annexed Korea on August 22, 1910.

[10] The most startling growth occurred during and after the World War, when Japan's trade passed the ¥4,000 million mark.

Eastern Inner Mongolia affecting railways, mines, opening of new treaty ports, leasing of land, and appointment of advisers to the local Chinese authorities; and admitted certain prior rights of Japan in connection with exploitation of the Hanyehping coal and iron mines near Hankow.[11] Japanese naval vessels also occupied the German islands lying north of the equator in the South Seas. Secret agreements, signed with Britain, France, Russia and Italy in February-March 1917, allocated these gains to Japan in the settlement which was to follow the war. In 1918, finally, large numbers of Japanese troops spread over eastern Siberia, and remained there after troops of the allied and associated powers had been withdrawn.

Through most of this period, the United States was the only Western power with sufficient freedom of action to place restraint on Japan's advances in the Far East. When the terms of the Twenty-one Demands became known, Secretary Bryan sent identic notes to China and Japan, declaring that the American government could not "recognize any agreement or undertaking . . . impairing the treaty rights of the United States and its citizens in China, the political or territorial integrity of the Republic of China, or the international policy relative to China commonly known as the open door policy."[12] American diplomatic pressure was mainly responsible for securing withdrawal of Group V of the Twenty-one Demands which would have subjected the Chinese central government to a large measure of Japanese control. It could not prevent signature of the treaties of May 25, 1915, embodying most of the other demands. The protests were made independently of any other power, and were not backed by any form of military or naval pressure. The American navy, indeed, was exceptionally weak at the outset of the war; only later was a large naval building program authorized and pushed to completion. Essentially, the American government reserved the right to deal with the new situation created in the Far East at some later and more opportune time.

After the United States became a belligerent, its position *vis-à-vis* Japan was even more difficult. Japan capitalized on this situation by despatching Viscount Ishii to the United States as an envoy on special mission. The Lansing-Ishii agreement of November 2, 1917, while stressing Japan's adherence to the

[11] MacMurray, cited, Vol. II, pp. 1216-30.
[12] *Foreign Relations of the United States, 1915*, p. 146.

open door doctrine, lent strength to the Japanese case by admitting that territorial propinquity created "special interests" for the latter in China.[13] At the peace conference President Wilson, confronted with the secret treaties, was forced to permit transfer of the former German rights in Shantung province to Japan, while the German islands in the north Pacific went to Japan in the shape of a Class C mandate. Efforts by the Chinese delegation to induce reconsideration of Japan's gains in Manchuria under the 1915 treaties met with scant attention at the conference.

In the 1919-21 period, after negotiation of the Versailles Treaty, underlying weaknesses in Japan's position gradually became apparent. The Chinese delegates refused to sign the treaty. Explosive student outbursts drove the Japanese-dominated Anfu clique from office in Peking. The student uprising then passed into a broad nationalist movement, culminating in an effective boycott of Japanese goods. As the intervention in Siberia became less tenable, it tended to discredit the military in the eyes of the Japanese people. By early 1921 the moderate elements, who were to dominate a succession of Cabinets in Japan during the twenties, had become vocal and assertive. External factors in the balance of forces had also shifted against Japan. In the United States, the Shantung award became an issue that contributed to eventual rejection of the whole peace settlement. American naval expansion approached its peak during these years. The combined costs of the Siberian intervention and the naval race had become a heavy burden on Japan. The attitude of the European powers was also changing. Great Britain, in particular, was under pressure from Canada not to renew the Anglo-Japanese Alliance, which was about to expire. The cautious policy pursued by the American government since August 1914 had at last borne fruit. On July 27, 1921, President Harding extended invitations for the Washington Conference. It met under very different conditions from those which had prevailed at Paris two years earlier.

Agreements reached at Washington, of which the most important were signed on February 6, 1922, marked the conclusion of the period of Far Eastern crisis initiated by the World War. A broad compromise, involving naval armament and political questions, was effected between Japan and the Western

[13] *Foreign Relations of the United States, 1917,* pp. 264-5.

powers. The 5-5-3 naval ratio in capital ships and airplane carriers, established for Britain, the United States and Japan, relieved the latter of the heavy financial burden entailed by the naval building race. It also secured Japan against single-handed attack by Britain or the United States, especially in conjunction with the provision maintaining the *status quo* on fortifications and naval bases in a wide radius of the Pacific. The Four-Power Treaty, which pledged Britain, France, the United States and Japan to respect each other's insular possessions in the Pacific, supplanted the Anglo-Japanese Alliance.

In return for these substantial contributions to its security in Far Eastern waters, Japan withdrew from its advanced positions on the Asiatic continent and accepted a comprehensive redefinition of the open door policy in China. Assisted by neutral observers, the Chinese and Japanese delegates engaged in negotiations which led to an agreement restoring Shantung province to China. During the conference Japan also stated that it intended to evacuate Siberia when conditions permitted—a declaration carried out in 1922. In the Nine-Power Treaty Japan pledged itself, along with the other signatories, to respect China's sovereignty, independence and territorial and administrative integrity, to provide China the fullest and most unembarrassed opportunity to develop and maintain an effective and stable government, to uphold the principle of the open door throughout China, and not to take or support any action designed to create spheres of interest or exclusive rights in any region of China.[14]

If the territorial status existing in the Far East after this settlement is compared with that of August 1914, it will be seen that Japan's position had measurably improved. Its larger ambitions in Shantung and Siberia had not been attained. Yet it was now the mandatory power for the north Pacific islands, which were of immense strategic, if not economic, importance. In addition, Japan had radically strengthened its grip on South Manchuria. During the conference sessions, the Chinese delegates launched a determined attack on the validity of the Sino-Japanese treaties, including those applying to Manchuria, signed in May 1915 as a result of the Twenty-one Demands. On this issue, the Japanese delegates were adamant. Japan clung firmly

[14] For texts of treaties and resolutions, see *Conference on the Limitation of Armament*, pp. 1569-1659.

to its new treaty rights in Manchuria, and the conference failed to restore the pre-war status.

From the point of view of American Far Eastern policy, the Nine-Power Treaty was the most significant result of the conference. It secured, for the first time, formal and complete international acceptance of the open door principle as applied to China, defined in terms more concrete and comprehensive than ever before. On the other hand, the conference failed to establish satisfactory international machinery for the application or enforcement of the pledges taken under the Nine-Power Treaty. The treaty itself provided merely that when, in the opinion of a signatory, a situation had arisen involving application of the treaty's stipulations and rendering discussion of such application desirable, there should be "full and frank communication" between the contracting powers concerned. Resolution IV, providing for a Board of Reference of the treaty signatories to be set up in China for investigation and mediation of disputes, was emasculated by exceptions taken by certain powers at the conference and in the end the projected board was never established. No enforcement machinery was envisaged. With virtually unrestricted supremacy in Far Eastern waters, Japan was placed in a position where it might disregard the stipulations of the treaty with impunity. Short of combined Anglo-American action, which might prove difficult to secure at any given time, there was no assurance that independent action by Japan could be curbed. In this connection, a further important hiatus in the peace machinery of the Pacific, as established at Washington, should not be overlooked. Aside from Japan, only one other power—the U.S.S.R.—enjoyed similar advantages of geographical propinquity to China. Yet the Soviet Union was not invited to the Washington Conference, and did not become a signatory of the Nine-Power Treaty.

Ad Interim: 1922-1931

The Far Eastern *détente* which succeeded the Washington Conference bore remarkable similarities to the period after the Portsmouth Treaty. The settlement at Portsmouth had concluded the era of sharp, international conflict, marked by constant resort to arms, which had begun in 1895. It was followed by nearly ten years of relative peace, from September 5, 1905 to August 4, 1914. While international rivalries in China persisted during this period, they were not its most prominent feature. Revolutionary movements in China, culminating in the overthrow of the Manchu Dynasty, held the center of the stage. This cycle was now repeated under new circumstances. The post-war stabilization in the Far East, following the 1914-22 period of international conflict,[15] also lasted for nearly ten years, from February 6, 1922 to September 18, 1931. International rivalries were again subordinated to revolutionary developments in China, marking a new and higher stage of the latter's efforts to achieve domestic stability and modernization and freedom from international servitudes.

Before considering this central aspect of the 1922-31 era, several important events in Japanese-American relations should be noted. On April 14, 1923 an exchange of notes between Secretary Hughes and the Japanese Ambassador, Masanao Hanihara, declared that the Lansing-Ishii agreement, in view of the understandings reached at the Washington Conference, should be considered "as cancelled and of no further force or effect."[16] In September of that year the great earthquake occurred at Tokyo and its environs; it was marked by an extraordinary response from the United States, both in sympathy and material aid. Nine months later, on May 26, 1924, the American Congress passed the statute barring aliens "ineligible to citizenship" from admission to the United States. President Coolidge addressed formal objection to Congress against passage of this statute, but to no avail.[17] The act was accepted with restraint by the authorities in Japan, but its implications sank deep into the Japanese consciousness and tended to counteract the reorientation of Japan's foreign policy which the moderates were seeking to achieve. Two further events deserve notice. In 1929 Japan adhered to the Paris Pact, while in 1930, at the London Naval Conference, Japan accepted extension of the naval limitation principle to cruisers, destroyers and submarines. The bitter struggle in Japan over ratification of this latter agreement presaged the rise of a militant opposition to the moderate ele-

[15] This period of armed strife was actually concluded by withdrawal of Japanese military forces from Siberia in October 1922.

[16] U. S. Senate, *Treaties, Conventions, International Agreements: 1910-1923*, Vol. III, pp. 3825-6.

[17] For analysis of the immigration issue and documentary texts, see Raymond Leslie Buell, *Japanese Immigration*, World Peace Foundation Pamphlets, Vol. VII, Nos. 5-6, pp. 281-380.

ments which had mainly directed Japanese policy in the preceding decade.

The dominant issues in Far Eastern politics during this era, however, centered about the upheaval that was occurring in China. Vigorous nationalist forces, unleashed in China immediately after the World War, persisted throughout the era of post-war stabilization. Underlying the domestic strife and turmoil, and continually reappearing in one form or another, was a powerful drive for emancipation from the semi-colonial status imposed by the unequal treaties. The opening breach in this system was made by the Versailles Treaty, which had deprived Germany and Austria-Hungary of their concessions and special treaty privileges in China. In 1921-4 the Soviet Union had voluntarily relinquished similar privileges formerly possessed by Russia, except for rights and interests connected with the Chinese Eastern Railway in North Manchuria. Most of the leading countries and many lesser powers, however, still exercised various special privileges under the unequal treaty system. These included territorial and administrative rights in concessions, settlements and leaseholds, the extraterritorial system, the statutory tariff, navigation of China's coastal and inland waters by foreign naval and commercial vessels, and garrisoning of foreign military and naval units in Shanghai, Peking, Tientsin and at certain other points.

China's first determined effort to overthrow this system occurred during the revolutionary upheaval of 1925-7. The struggle continued in a more moderate form under the Nanking Government which emerged in 1927-8. Between 1925 and 1931, the brunt of the offensive shifted from one power to another; at different times Great Britain, the Soviet Union and Japan felt the weight of this Chinese drive for a national status of equality and independence. The Kuomintang, or Nationalist Party, reorganized and strengthened by an *entente* with the U.S.S.R. established by Sun Yat-sen in 1923, after rebuffs from the Western powers, was the moving force behind the rapid developments of these years.

From 1925 to 1927 the nationalist attack was directed mainly against Great Britain, especially at Hongkong and Hankow; British policy, however, despite precautionary mobilization of troops at Shanghai in 1927, was markedly restrained. Under the conciliatory policy of Foreign Minister Shidehara, Japan stood aloof from the conflict during this period; the Japanese gunboats, in a notable example of restraint, refrained from participating in the bombardment laid down by foreign gunboats at Nanking in March 1927. This attitude changed as the Kuomintang forces, now under control of the Chinese conservatives, entered the northern provinces in 1927 and 1928. A new Cabinet, dominated by General Baron Tanaka, dispatched Japanese expeditionary forces to Shantung in the spring of 1927 and again in May 1928. At Tsinan, in the latter case, these forces clashed with units of General Chiang Kai-shek's Nationalist troops. The "positive" policy of General Tanaka was also evidenced by a series of warnings against carrying the war into Manchuria, by suspicious circumstances attending the death of Chang Tso-lin at Mukden in June 1928, by pressure on Chang Hsueh-liang against adhering to the Nationalist cause, and by maintenance of occupationary forces in Shantung, despite a severe Chinese boycott of Japanese goods occasioned thereby, until the spring of 1929. The turn of the Soviet Union came in the autumn of 1929, with a series of raids on Chinese Eastern Railway establishments and arrests of Soviet officials connected with the railway, on the ground that they were engaging in Communist propaganda. A sharp clash between Soviet and Chinese military forces in North Manchuria quickly led to an agreement restoring the *status quo ante,* but not before Secretary Stimson's effort to invoke the Paris Pact had been rebuffed by Moscow.

The results of this nationalist insurgence were recorded in a series of important diplomatic achievements, which, from 1927 to 1931, forced the second great breach in the unequal treaty system. Early in 1927, Great Britain agreed to restore the British concessions at Hankow and Kiukiang to Chinese jurisdiction. Other agreements followed, until by 1930 China had also regained concessions at Chinkiang and Amoy, the Belgian concession at Tientsin, and the British leasehold of Weihaiwei. The tariff and extraterritoriality conferences proposed by the Washington Conference had met in China in 1926, but, except for approving a slight increase in the tariff rates, had accomplished little toward restoring Chinese sovereignty in customs and judicial matters. On July 25, 1928, however, the United States signed a treaty with the Nanking Government providing for tariff equality by January 1, 1929, subject to a most-favored-nation proviso. The State Department rightly judged that this lead would be followed by the other powers. In the summer and fall of 1928 the Chinese government concluded a series of similar treaties with the several powers; after a year's delay, occasioned by Japanese hesitation, China achieved tariff autonomy early in 1930.[18] Another significant demand in this drive toward equality of status—abolition of the extraterritorial system—was also being vigorously pushed by the Chinese authorities. Eventually, only four major powers, France, Great Britain, the United States and Japan, blocked the path toward restoration of China's judicial autonomy. In the summer of 1931, with new legal codes prepared and partially functioning, this effort stood on the verge of success. Negotiations with Britain and the United States had reached a stage at which the basic issue was already conceded; details regarding the status of Shanghai during a transitional period were all that remained to be settled. Before final agreement was consummated, the events at Mukden on the night of September 18 supervened.

These developments in China were of prime significance for American Far Eastern policy. The open door doctrine looks forward, at least by implication, to the day when China will establish control in its own house. It is applicable, on the political side, as a self-denying principle until this end is achieved. Once China has attained full and independent mastery over its national destinies, the covenants of the Nine-Power Treaty will be superseded and the political aspects of the open door doctrine—now, perhaps, the leading factor in America's involvement in the Far East—will lapse.

Within the decade of the twenties, China had made rapid advances in both the internal and external spheres. Some of the most backward of the old regional warlords had been eliminated, and a promising start toward modernization of the administrative services had been made. The handling of the national finances, though much still remained to be done, had also improved. A certain degree of centralization of government had been achieved. Despite this progress, the fundamental task of overcoming the old-established elements of disunity, instability and weakness had not been accomplished. When Marshal Chang Hsueh-liang of Manchuria threw in his lot with the Nationalist authorities at Nanking in December 1928, China

[18] Subject to a three-year conventional schedule on Japan's major items of export to China.

was more united than at any previous time since the collapse of the Manchu Dynasty in 1911. This unity, however, was still more nominal than real. In 1929 there was a brief, but important, clash near Hankow, in which the forces of Generals Pai Chung-hsi and Li Tsung-jen were defeated and forced to withdraw into Kwangsi. In 1930 there was a large-scale civil war between the Nationalist authorities at Nanking, under Chiang Kai-shek, and the coalition headed by Generals Feng Yu-hsiang and Yen Hsi-shan in North China. In May 1931 a split at Nanking led to establishment of a rival government at Canton; later in the year, an armed clash between these governments seemed imminent. The protracted struggle between the Nanking Government and the Chinese Communist forces had already assumed large proportions in 1930-1. Largely by reason of this failure to establish effective political unity, China fell short of achieving its untrammelled independence during these years. A long period of severe struggle lay ahead before an equally favorable opportunity for the realization of this aim would present itself.

CHAPTER II

THE MANCHURIAN CRISIS: 1931-1933

The autumn of 1931 ushered in a third cycle of acute international conflict in the Far East. One important feature marks it off from the previous crises. After eight years of almost unremitting tension, it has produced no large-scale, overt collision between the major foreign powers. It has continued nominally as a struggle between China and Japan alone. Although the interests of the foreign powers, including the United States, have been more and more seriously affected, they have offered no direct and forceful challenge to Japan's advance. Yet this third cycle of Far Eastern conflict is by no means over; on the contrary, all indications point to the fact that its climax—and the ultimate decision—may still be reserved for some time to come.

Under the circumstances which prevailed at the end of 1931, Japan possessed greater freedom of action than at any time since the World War. The European powers and the United States were preoccupied by the effects of an economic crisis which was still in full swing. England's abandonment of the gold standard virtually coincided with the Mukden "incident" of September 18. While British and American naval construction had lagged since 1922, Japan had steadily built up to treaty limits, thus reinforcing its dominance in Far Eastern waters. The U.S.S.R. was absorbed in the tasks of the first five-year plan, agricultural collectivization was only beginning, and the defenses of the Siberian maritime provinces were relatively undeveloped. China was in the throes of civil strife, and the Yangtze Valley provinces were suffering from a disastrous flood. These conditions were of such a kind that they could not for the most part be easily or quickly modified, while after 1933 the rise of Nazi Germany prolonged and intensified the political disturbances in Europe.

The first phase of the renewed Far Eastern unsettlement, ending with the Tangku Truce of May 31, 1933, was covered almost exactly by the last eighteen months of Secretary Stimson's term of office. From the outset the State Department co-ordinated its diplomatic efforts with those of the League Council, in an attempt to localize the hostilities in Manchuria. As early as September 24 the American government dispatched identic notes to China and Japan, similar in tenor to telegrams sent by the President of the League of Nations two days earlier. On October 5 Secretary Stimson telegraphed a statement to the Secretary-General of the League, declaring that the American Government would act "independently through its diplomatic representatives" in the endeavor "to reinforce what the League does . . ."[1] For several months the State Department, working on the assumption that the hands of the moderates at Tokyo should be strengthened, confined its independent action mainly to a series of unpublished diplomatic protests.[2] During this period two American representatives participated informally in the League deliberations. On December 10, 1931 the League Commission of Inquiry, which included an American national, Major-General Frank R. McCoy, in its personnel, was appointed. The Minseito Cabinet resigned on the following day. Japanese military operations in Manchuria continued to spread, and on January 7, 1932 Secretary Stimson issued his non-recognition statement.

Couched in terms very nearly identical with Secretary Bryan's note of May 11, 1915, this statement enlarged the scope of the earlier move by attempting to secure universal application of the non-recognition doctrine as a sanction to the Pact of Paris. Its essential section declared that the American government "cannot admit the legality of any situation *de facto* nor does it intend to recognize any treaty or agreement entered into between those Governments, or agents thereof, which may impair the treaty rights of the United States or its citizens in China, including those which relate to the sovereignty, the independence, or the territorial and administrative integrity of the Republic of China, or to the international policy relative to China, commonly known as the open-door policy; and that it does not intend to recognize any situation, treaty, or agreement which may be brought about by means contrary to the covenants and obligations of the Pact of Paris of August 27, 1928, to which

[1] Henry L. Stimson, *The Far Eastern Crisis,* p. 52.

[2] Eventually published in "Conditions in Manchuria," Senate Document 53, 72nd Congress, 1st Session.

treaty both China and Japan, as well as the United States, are parties."[3]

The terms of this note were communicated in advance to the British and French Ambassadors, and the co-operation of their governments was invited. The force of the *démarche*, however, was blunted by the cool reception accorded it at London. A Foreign Office *communiqué*, published on January 11, underlined Japanese assurances respecting the open door in Manchuria and indicated that, in view of these statements, "his Majesty's Government have not considered it necessary to address any formal note to the Japanese Government on the lines of the American Government's note. . . ."[4] On the same day, an editorial in *The Times* stated that "in declining to address a communication to the Chinese and Japanese Governments on the lines of Mr. Stimson's Note, the British Government have acted wisely."

The State Department's inclination, following upon the Shanghai hostilities, to clarify the position through a statement issued by the several Nine-Power Treaty signatories was also balked when Secretary Stimson became convinced, after a number of telephone conversations with Sir John Simon, that the British Government was "reluctant to join in such a *démarche*."[5] At this period American public opinion, stirred by the bombings of Chapei, tended to be responsive to a lead given by the government. Under the circumstances, Secretary Stimson was compelled to confine this action to a unilateral statement of the American position, given on February 24, 1932 in his letter to Senator Borah. In this letter, after recapitulating the historical steps in the formulation of American Far Eastern policy and its embodiment in the Nine-Power Treaty, he declared:

"This treaty thus represents a carefully developed and matured international policy intended, on the one hand, to assure to all of the contracting parties their rights and interests in and with regard to China and on the other hand, to assure to the people of China the fullest opportunity to develop without molestation their sovereignty and independence according to the modern and enlightened standards believed to maintain among the peoples of this earth. At the time this treaty was

[3] State Department, *Press Releases*, January 9, 1932, pp. 41-2.
[4] Arnold J. Toynbee, *Survey of International Affairs*, 1932, pp. 541-2.
[5] Stimson, *The Far Eastern Crisis*, p. 164.

signed, it was known that China was engaged in an attempt to develop the free institutions of a self-governing republic after her recent revolution from an autocratic form of government; that she would require many years of both economic and political effort to that end; and that her progress would necessarily be slow. The treaty was thus a covenant of self-denial among the signatory powers in deliberate renunciation of any policy of aggression which might tend to interfere with that development. It was believed—and the whole history of the development of the 'open door' policy reveals that faith—that only by such a process, under the protection of such an agreement, could the fullest interests not only of China but of all nations which have intercourse with her best be served. . . .

"It must be remembered also that this treaty was one of several treaties and agreements entered into at the Washington Conference by the various powers concerned, all of which were interrelated and interdependent. No one of these treaties can be disregarded without disturbing the general understanding and equilibrium which were intended to be accomplished and effected by the group of agreements arrived at in their entirety. The Washington Conference was essentially a disarmament conference, aimed to promote the possibility of peace in the world not only through the cessation of competition in naval armament but also by the solution of various other disturbing problems which threatened the peace of the world, particularly in the Far East. These problems were all interrelated. The willingness of the American Government to surrender its then commanding lead in battleship construction and to leave its positions at Guam and in the Philippines without further fortification, was predicated upon, among other things, the self-denying covenants contained in the Nine Power Treaty, which assured the nations of the world not only of equal opportunity for their Eastern trade but also against the military aggrandizement of any other power at the expense of China. One can not discuss the possibility of modifying or abrogating those provisions of the Nine Power Treaty without considering at the same time the other promises upon which they were really dependent. . . .

"On January 7th last, upon the instruction of the President, this Government formally notified Japan and China that it would not recognize any situation, treaty, or agreement entered into by those Governments in violation of the covenants of these treaties, which affected the rights of our Government or its citizens in China. If a similar decision should be reached and a similar position taken by the other governments of the world, a caveat will be placed upon such action which, we believe, will effectively bar the legality hereafter of any title or right sought to be obtained by pressure or treaty violation, and which, as has been shown by history in the past, will eventually lead to the restoration to China of rights and titles of which she may have been deprived. . . ."

This letter, as the commentary in Secretary Stimson's book indicates, was in part directed toward the approaching session of the League Assembly. Its open invitation for international action was accepted by the Assembly on March 11, 1932, when it adopted a resolution including a provision declaring it incumbent on League members "not to recognize any situation, treaty or agreement which may be brought about by means contrary to the Covenant of the League of Nations." Nearly a year elapsed before the Lytton Report was completed, presented to the League Council, and made the basis of a formal report. On February 24, 1933, in its report approving the recommendations of the Lytton Commission, the Assembly included a provision obligating League members not to recognize Manchukuo.

One week later the Hoover administration went out of office. Its Far Eastern policy was based on traditional lines, both in the principles advocated and the cautious methods of action used to uphold them. In one respect, the extent and closeness of its co-operation with the League of Nations, the State Department had broken new ground. On the whole, however, the failure of Washington and London to see eye to eye at critical moments had nullified the effectiveness of this co-operation. The nonrecognition doctrine, even though broadened into an international sanction of the Nine-Power Treaty, the Pact of Paris and the League Covenant, was unable to effect an immediate reversal of the results of aggression so long as it remained unsupported by more effective measures than the force of public opinion. General acceptance of the doctrine, nevertheless, by preventing Japan from securing legal title to the gains which it had achieved, left the question open for ultimate determination. This, too, was a much stronger reservation than the United States, acting alone and against its allies, had been able to interpose during the World War.

CHAPTER III

JAPANESE PRESSURE ON RESURGENT CHINA: 1933-1937

A second phase of the current Far Eastern crisis, in which issues affecting American policy were less sharply emphasized, lies between the Tangku Truce (May 31, 1933) and the Lukouchiao "incident" (July 7, 1937). In Manchukuo, during these four years, Japan consolidated its military-political control, and carried forward an economic program featuring railway construction and the development of heavy industry. Japanese pressure of varying intensity was also directed against China south of the Wall throughout this period, but without giving rise to large-scale hostilities. Pressure was also felt to some extent at Nanking, where a tariff revision favoring Japanese products, for example, was secured in 1934. The Nanking authorities further sought to comply with the demand for rigid limitations on anti-Japanese agitation in the press and on the public platform. On the whole, however, the Chinese central government managed to stave off full application of Japan's larger aims, as embodied in the so-called Hirota "three principles," particularly with respect to recognition of Manchukuo and establishment of a Japan-China-Manchukuo economic bloc.

Mainly as the result of successive steps in 1935 and 1936, Japan's economic-political penetration achieved much greater progress in North China. In accordance with the terms of the Ho-Umetsu and Chin-Doihara agreements of June 1935, extorted by threat of military action, the troops and party organs of the central government were driven from Hopei and Chahar provinces. This process was carried still further by the five-province "autonomy" movement conducted by Major-General Kenji Doihara in the fall of 1935. Although its full objective was not attained, the movement led to the formation of the semi-autonomous Hopei-Chahar Political Council, with Japanese military, political and economic advisers. In addition, there was set up in the former East Hopei "demilitarized zone" a regime, headed by Yin Ju-keng, which was definitely subordinated to Japanese control. Within this area, and along its coasts, Chinese customs authority was overridden, and a large smuggling traffic in Japanese goods, which had previously developed, was given quasi-legality by low tariff rates imposed by the new East Hopei authorities. In December 1935, on the heels of the "autonomy" agitation, a considerable area of Chahar province was occupied by Chinese and Mongol puppet forces. Efforts to extend this occupation of Inner Mongolia failed. When similar puppet forces invaded Suiyuan province in November 1936, they were defeated by local provincial troops under General Fu Tso-yi. Economic penetration, aside from growing Japanese influence in Tientsin, notably in the taking over of bankrupted Chinese textile mills, was furthered by agreements affecting railway projects, airlines, mining rights, and stimulation of cotton cultivation. These latter agreements were obtained under duress, and it proved difficult to apply them in practice. Complete Japanese control in North China, either in the political or economic fields, was far from being achieved—a fact which became increasingly obvious in 1936 and early 1937.

Toward the end of this period, under the stimulus of revived nationalist forces, China's political unification began to make substantial progress. The student demonstrations at Peiping in December 1935, which rapidly spread throughout the country, were soon transformed into a broad movement for national unity and resistance to Japanese aggression. Both the central authorities and the dissident groups felt the pressure exerted by this movement. During the summer of 1936, after a threatened clash in the south had been averted, there were significant results: reassertion of the central government's authority in Kwangtung province, and establishment of co-operative relations between Nanking and the Kwangsi leaders, Pai Chung-hsi and Li Tsung-jen. From December 1936 to February 1937, as a result of the fortnight's detention of Chiang Kai-shek at Sian, the possibility of civil war again emerged. The net results of this crisis, however, were the institution of negotiations for a Kuomintang-Communist united front, and the incorporation of Chang Hsueh-liang's Manchurian troops into the central army. By the late spring of 1937, the authority of the central government was acknowledged by every important political and military group in China.

Economic reconstruction was taking place along lines which tended to strengthen and consolidate political unity. China's commercial airlines were spreading a network of rapid communication throughout the country. Highway construction proceeded steadily, and bus services were expanding. New railways, notably the final link connecting Hankow and Canton, were being laid down. With respect to the basic issue of land reform, little more than tentative experiments of a local character had yet been inaugurated. On the other hand, the reorganization of state finances was making real progress. Central revenues had nearly doubled since 1929, despite the loss of Manchuria and the effects of smuggling in North China. Two-thirds of the old domestic loan issues had been refunded, and successive consolidations of new issues effected. Settlements of a majority of defaulted foreign loans were negotiated, and payments in arrears were being made. The acute economic crisis of 1934-5 had yielded to the significant currency reform promulgated on November 3, 1935. This reform, which nationalized silver and instituted a managed paper currency, proved to be a pronounced success. Later agreements with the American Treasury, providing dollar exchange for China's silver, placed the new currency on a sound basis and overcame the previous untoward effects of the American silver purchase policy on the Chinese economy. By the middle of 1937 Chinese business and foreign trade were regaining the high levels reached six or seven years earlier. Quotations of Chinese external bonds were nearly double those ruling a decade before, and new foreign loans were being secured. Both in the political and economic spheres, sound foundations had been laid for a stable and assured advance of more far-reaching proportions.

At the outset of this period, the Roosevelt administration had effected a considerable shift of emphasis in the Far Eastern policy of the United States. While the American government still continued to uphold the principles of the Washington Conference settlement, it relegated any positive action even further to the background. Fewer protests were registered at Tokyo, and efforts to secure co-operative measures against Japanese aggression sharply diminished. There were several reasons for this change of emphasis. The new administration was even more absorbed in coping with the domestic problems created by the depression than its predecessor. After May 1933, with overt

Sino-Japanese hostilities giving way to less startling and provocative methods of conflict, the attention of the world was no longer centered on the Far East. In any case, except possibly for the brief period of the Shanghai hostilities early in 1932, it was doubtful whether American public opinion would have supported aggressively sanctionist measures against Japan. The growing European political crisis now made it less than ever possible for the League of Nations to take positive action in the Far East. Under the circumstances, the American government continued to make occasional statements for the diplomatic record, as well as maintaining the non-recognition doctrine. Essentially, it fell back on long-term methods of restoring the Far Eastern equilibrium which Japan had upset. These efforts, exemplified by inauguration of a naval construction program designed to reach treaty limits by 1942, were mainly independent in character. They did not exclude co-operative action wherever possible, as during the course of the naval negotiations at London. The agreement of November 16, 1933, establishing diplomatic relations with the U.S.S.R., also contributed toward weighing the balance. While immediate results were not expected to flow from this defensive action, the field was not abandoned. American Far Eastern policy had returned to the position adopted in 1915-21.

On taking office, the Roosevelt administration was immediately faced with the necessity of determining its attitude toward Manchukuo. At the end of February 1933, the League Assembly had invited the United States to co-operate with the Far Eastern Advisory Committee of twenty-one nations, established to facilitate settlement of the Sino-Japanese dispute in conformity with the recommendations of its Manchurian report. This invitation was accepted on March 11, when Mr. Hugh R. Wilson, American Minister to Switzerland, was appointed to participate in the Committee's deliberations in a non-voting capacity.[1] At the very outset, the new administration had thus officially indicated its continued support of the non-recognition doctrine. In June 1933 the Advisory Committee recommended certain routine steps affecting enforcement of the non-recognition of Manchukuo. These recommendations, with a few exceptions, were approved by the American government.

[1] Texts of invitation and response in State Department *Press Releases,* March 18, 1933, pp. 175-8.

During these months, the Sino-Japanese hostilities which led to signature of the Tangku Truce were occurring in North China. If American diplomatic protests were delivered in Tokyo at this time, they were not made public. The first sharp issue handled by Secretary Hull developed over the Amau statement of April 17, 1934. In this declaration, the Tokyo Foreign Office spokesman claimed for Japan the right to act single-handedly in maintaining "peace and order in Eastern Asia." He declared that "any joint operations undertaken by foreign powers, even in the name of technical and financial assistance" to China, were "bound to acquire political significance." Specifically, Japan would oppose "supplying China with war planes, building airdromes in China, and detailing military instructors or military advisers to China or contracting a loan to provide funds for political uses."[2]

The terms of this pronouncement affected not only technical assistance being rendered to China by a number of League advisers, but were so drawn as to call into question certain American economic and political relationships with China. In May 1933 the Reconstruction Finance Corporation had granted a three-year, 50-million-dollar wheat and cotton credit to the Chinese government. American firms were participating in the development of commercial aviation in China. Toward the end of 1933 the Curtiss-Wright Corporation announced plans for the construction of a five-million-dollar airplane assembly plant in China, designed to produce military planes, which was set up at Hangchow early in 1934. In 1932-3, moreover, the Aeronautics Trade Division of the Commerce Department co-operated with American aircraft firms in the selection of a number of American aviation officers, who assisted in establishing training schools for Chinese pilots at Hangchow and Canton.[3] The sale of American aircraft and accessories to China, including military planes, had risen from $157,515 in 1932 to $1,762,-247 in 1933.

On April 25 a British inquiry concerning the Amau statement was made at Tokyo; four days later, the American Ambassador delivered a note to the Japanese Foreign Minister. As

[2] Text as cited by Arnold J. Toynbee, *Survey of International Affairs, 1934,* pp. 650-1.

[3] U. S. Senate, *Hearings Before the Special Committee Investigating the Munitions Industry,* Part 6, Exhibits 551-7; also pp. 1445-52.

published in substance by the State Department on April 30, this communication stated:

"Recent indications of attitude on the part of the Japanese Government" with reference to China, coming from "sources so authoritative as to preclude their being ignored," makes it necessary for the American government to "reaffirm the position of the United States with regard to questions of rights and interests involved." The United States is "associated with China or with Japan or with both, together with certain other countries, in multilateral treaties relating to rights and obligations in the Far East, and in one great multilateral treaty to which practically all the countries of the world are parties. Treaties can lawfully be modified or terminated only by processes prescribed or recognized or agreed upon by the parties to them. . . . In the opinion of the American people and the American government, no nation can, without the assent of the other nations concerned, rightfully endeavor to make conclusive its will in situations where there are involved the rights, the obligations, and the legitimate interests of other sovereign states."[4]

No reply was made to this communication, and there the matter was allowed to rest. Some of the American relationships with China listed above have since lapsed, while others have continued. In April 1935 the Chinese government canceled the 50-million-dollar credit agreement, apparently owing to inability to dispose of the wheat and cotton in China; of the total amount, only $17,105,385 was used. Two months later the contract of the American aviation instructors at the Hangchow training school expired and was not renewed. On April 1, 1935 Pan American Airways acquired the American share in the China National Aviation Corporation, and this interest has been continued. The Curtiss-Wright airplane plant has latterly been transferred from Hangchow to the interior of China, where it is still producing military planes for the Chinese government. Sales of American aircraft and accessories to China, principally military planes, have continued throughout the recent period.

The broad challenge to the open door policy, laid down by the Amau statement for China as a whole, was driven home more effectively in Manchukuo. After 1932 Japanese investments in Manchuria greatly increased while other foreign capital tended to withdraw, as evidenced by the closing of foreign

[4] State Department, *Press Releases,* May 5, 1934, pp. 244-5.

banking, trading and construction concerns. The most important controversial issue developed over the oil monopoly law promulgated by the Manchukuo authorities in November 1934 and made effective on April 10, 1935. On several occasions the American government, as well as Great Britain and the Netherlands, protested to Japan against the application of this law, but to no effect. By 1936 the Standard-Vacuum Oil Company, the Asiatic Petroleum Company and the Texas Oil Company had all closed their branches and retired from the profitable field of oil distribution in Manchuria, which they had previously controlled. The smuggling operations in North China, facilitated by the establishment of Yin Ju-keng's East Hopei "autonomous" regime in November 1935, also constituted an infringement of the open door policy. At its height, the illicit trade curtailed China's tariff receipts, reduced imports from Western countries, and undermined the security of foreign loans hypothecated on the Chinese customs revenue. Protests made by the British and American governments at Tokyo, however, were entirely ineffective.

The Amau statement had afforded a glimpse of Japan's ultimate objectives in China, even though it had not been enforced. Secretary Hull's rejoinder showed that the American government was still intent on maintaining unrestricted economic access of its citizens to China. The results in this case, compared with the course of events in Manchukuo and East Hopei, demonstrated once more that the open door policy could only be upheld in areas over which China exerted effective administrative control.

Issues affecting China's territorial and administrative integrity came prominently to the fore in the spring of 1935, and again during the five-province "autonomy" movement in the autumn of that year. In the first instance, the American government made no public reference to the Japanese demands on the North China authorities, although press reports indicated that secret diplomatic protests may have been delivered at Tokyo. On December 5, 1935, however, after conferences between the British Ambassador and State Department officials, simultaneous declarations were made at Washington and London. The statement issued to the press by Secretary Hull declared:

"There is going on in and with regard to North China a political struggle which is unusual in character and which may have far-reaching effects . . . whatever the origin, whoever the agents, be what they may be the methods, the fact stands out that an effort is being made—and is being resisted—to bring about a substantial change in the political status and condition of several of China's northern Provinces. . . . In the area under reference . . . there are located, and our rights and obligations appertain to, a considerable number of American nationals, some American property and substantial American commercial and cultural activities. The American Government is closely observing what is happening there. . . . As I have stated on many occasions, it seems to this Government most important in this period of world-wide political unrest and economic instability that governments and peoples keep faith in principles and pledges. . . . This Government adheres to the provisions of the treaties to which it is a party and continues to bespeak respect for the provisions of treaties solemnly entered into for the purpose of facilitating and regulating, to reciprocal and common advantage, the contacts between and among the countries signatory."[5]

Secretary Hull's defense of the Nine-Power Treaty in this period was essentially restricted to the statements of April 1934 and December 1935. It was not designed to pass beyond a reaffirmation of American disagreement with Japan's actions, and a reservation of American treaty rights. It could not reverse the results of Japan's actions, that is, uphold the Nine-Power Treaty effectually by restoring the *status quo ante*. A successful challenge to this treaty, however, struck at the base of the Washington Conference system and rapidly undermined the treaty structure of the Pacific area. The naval limitation treaties, which had been achieved on the basis of a settlement of Far Eastern political questions, could not be maintained after that settlement had been repudiated by Japan. Collapse of naval limitation went hand in hand with the progressive inability to enforce the Nine-Power Treaty.

[5] State Department, *Press Releases*, December 7, 1935, pp. 487-8.

CHAPTER IV

COLLAPSE OF NAVAL LIMITATION

The first official reference to naval issues, following Japan's intervention in Manchuria, occurred in Secretary Stimson's letter to Senator Borah of February 1932. On the naval question, Secretary Stimson made the following points: (1) the several treaties and agreements entered into at Washington were "interrelated and interdependent;" (2) no one of these treaties could be disregarded without disturbing "the general understanding and equilibrium" intended to be achieved by the whole group of agreements; (3) at Washington the United States had surrendered its "commanding lead in battleship construction" and agreed to leave its "positions at Guam and in the Philippines without further fortification;" (4) these naval limitation commitments were predicated on the "self-denying covenants" of the Nine-Power Treaty.

Under this interpretation, the United States was logically entitled either to disavow the Washington naval treaties, or to demand an increased naval strength relative to Japan. The threat thus implied in Secretary Stimson's letter, however, did not impress Japan and was not carried into effect. During the next two years, in fact, the course of events led to a reversal of the respective American and Japanese roles which might be inferred from Secretary Stimson's statement. By 1934, when the issue of extending the naval limitation treaties became pressing, the United States was supporting an effort to maintain these agreements unimpaired. Japan, on the other hand, proved unwilling to accept a continuance of the ratio principle, whether because of *amour propre,* the exigencies of the internal political struggle, or the new responsibilities it had assumed in eastern Asia. By its military operations in China, Japan had effectively undermined the Nine-Power Treaty; eventually, by its denunciation of the Washington Naval Treaty, it was Japan which delivered the *coup de grace* to naval limitation.

Preliminary steps toward adequate replacement of over-age tonnage in the American Navy, after a long holiday of approximately ten years, were taken early in 1933, when the sum of $238,000,000 from P.W.A. funds was allotted to naval construction. In March 1934 the Navy Department secured authorization from Congress, in the Vinson-Trammell Act, to proceed with a naval building program designed to reach treaty limits by 1942. At this time, however, Congress passed no appropriations for actual construction. A statement issued by President Roosevelt on March 27, when he affixed his signature to the Vinson-Trammell Act, declared that the administration favored naval limitation and that actual construction under the act depended on the action of future Congresses.[1] This declaration, in view of the approaching expiry of the naval treaties, was apparently directed in part toward Japan. On several occasions since 1931, Japan had already given indications that it was prepared to challenge the Washington and London naval agreements. In December 1932 the Japanese delegates to the Disarmament Conference suggested the need for a higher ratio as against Britain and the United States and for stiff reductions in "offensive" vessels, particularly capital ships and aircraft carriers.[2] On May 25, 1933 Ambassador Sato served notice at Geneva that Japan was not prepared to accept renewal of the Washington-London treaties on the existing basis, since it regarded those treaties as "unstable."[3]

Japan's new orientation was expounded more fully at the naval conversations held in the autumn of 1934 at London in preparation for the 1935 conference. The Japanese delegation favored a "common upper limit" of global tonnage for all powers—essentially a demand for parity. In addition, they proposed abolition of "offensive" vessels, i.e., battleships, aircraft carriers and heavy cruisers, but not submarines—which were classed as "defensive." These latter proposals, which ran counter to certain British and American suggestions for reduction, received little consideration, since the Japanese delegation insisted on prior acceptance of its demand for parity before proceeding to discussion of more concrete aspects of the naval problem.

[1] *New York Times,* March 28, 1934.

[2] League of Nations, *Conference for the Limitation and Reduction of Armaments, 1932-33,* Conf. D. 150, December 9, 1932.

[3] *Ibid., Minutes of the General Commission,* Vol. II, pp. 504-5.

Neither Great Britain nor the United States, however, was prepared to abandon the ratio principle, and the conversations adjourned without result early in November. On December 29, 1934 Japan notified the United States of its intention to terminate the Washington Naval Treaty.[4] As the result of this notification, and failing conclusion of a new agreement, the naval limitation treaties were due to lapse on December 31, 1936.

After lengthy diplomatic negotiations, which for months seemed destined to prove unsuccessful, a full-dress naval conference including Britain, France, the United States, Japan and Italy finally opened at London in December 1935. At the first meeting, on December 9, the basic difficulty which had been revealed by the preparatory conversations again emerged. Japan clung firmly to its proposal for a "common upper limit" of naval tonnage, but was eventually confronted with united opposition from the other powers, including France and Italy. On January 15 the Japanese delegation formally withdrew from the conference. A new treaty, providing for advance notification of annual building programs and certain qualitative limitations, was signed by France, Britain and the United States on March 25, 1936. The ratio limitations opposed by Japan were entirely omitted from this treaty, but in June 1936 Japan announced its definite refusal to adhere.[5]

On December 31, 1936 the former limitations imposed by the Washington and London naval agreements lapsed, including the important provision (Article 19 of the Washington Naval Treaty) restricting fortifications in the Pacific. Thus far, except for minor proposals affecting expenditure for harbor improvements at Guam, Midway and Wake islands laid before Congress in 1939, the United States has not moved to take advantage of this freedom to strengthen the fortification of its island possessions in the Pacific. On the other hand, the American naval authorities have prepared plans envisaging ultimate fortification of Guam at an estimated cost rivaling British expenditure on the Singapore base. With government assistance, moreover, Pan American Airways has established a trans-Pacific commercial airline via Honolulu, Midway, Wake and Guam to Manila and Hongkong. A British-American condominium of Canton

[4] Text in State Department *Press Releases,* January 5, 1935, pp. 2-3.
[5] *New York Times,* June 30, 1936.

and Enderbury islands, arranged after some dispute occasioned by American occupation, also holds out the possibility of an eventual trans-Pacific airline to Australia from the United States.

In addition to these factors, some of which may possibly be observed with a degree of concern by Japan, the American naval building program is rapidly assuming the proportions reached during the World War period. The authorizations for naval construction in the Vinson-Trammel Act have been supported since 1935 by annual Congressional appropriations, and the contracts for these "treaty limit" vessels have been regularly awarded from year to year. On May 17, 1938 a naval expansion bill, providing a 20 per cent increase in the authorized strength of the navy, also became law. Meanwhile, in February 1938, Britain, France and the United States sought to obtain official assurances from Japan that the latter was not exceeding the limits on size and gun calibers of capital ships and cruisers fixed by the London Naval Treaty of 1936.[6] Failing in this attempt, the three Western powers exchanged notes terminating the qualitative limitations on capital ships contained in the 1936 treaty.[7] Several months later Britain and the United States agreed to limit the size of capital ships to 45,000 tons, with 16-inch guns. The first six capital ships laid down in the American replacement program did not exceed 35,000 tons; current naval appropriations for the fiscal year 1940, however, provide for two additional battleships displacing 45,000 tons.

The accompanying table indicates total American naval ex-

UNITED STATES NAVAL EXPENDITURE,
1932–1940*

Fiscal Years	*Total*	*New Construction*
1932..........	$357,617,833	$39,588,673
1933..........	349,561,924	48,319,748
1934..........	297,029,290	66,457,921
1935..........	436,447,860	132,738,634
1936..........	529,031,665	186,895,381
1937..........	548,801,242	187,910,529
1938..........	588,828,854	191,393,163
1939†.........	616,635,250	179,620,000
1940†.........	676,498,800	235,000,000

**The Budget of the United States Government, 1940*, pp. 921, A62.
† Estimated.

[6] For American note, see State Department *Press Releases*, February 5, 1938, pp. 223-6.
[7] *Ibid.*, April 2, 1938, pp. 437-8.

penditure, and the amounts spent for new construction, during recent years. For 1939 and 1940, the figures show estimated expenditures. Especially for 1940, however, it may be expected that these estimates will be considerably surpassed. Total naval appropriations for the 1940 fiscal year, including those in the second deficiency bill, come to slightly more than 800 million dollars.

CHAPTER V

JAPANESE-AMERICAN TRADE FRICTION, 1933-1936

During the first Roosevelt administration, a considerable degree of friction developed over trade issues between Japan and the United States. Japan's unusual export boom in these years coincided with a halting recovery of foreign trade in the rest of the world, and thus attracted special attention from competitors in Western countries. Although Great Britain felt the brunt of this competition in 1933-4, the outcry against Japanese competition spread to American manufacturers in 1934-5. Complaints from American industrialists were seconded by members of Congress, and articles on the Japanese trade "menace" appeared in the press. The usual charges of dumping, unfair trade practices, and export subsidies were leveled against Japan; none of these, however, represented important factors in Japan's trade expansion. More important was the influence of low wage costs, reinforced by competitive advantages deriving from managerial and technical progress, rationalization of industry, and depreciation of the yen.

Two issues were uppermost: first, Japanese inroads on the American market; and, second, Japanese competition with American products in the world market. Of these, the first created the greatest amount of friction.

The great bulk of Japan's exports to the United States during this period, as indicated in the accompanying table, were not strictly competitive by any legitimate standard. For the typical year 1934, approximately 70 per cent of American imports from Japan was non-dutiable, consisting of commodities either not produced in the United States, such as raw silk, or entirely supplementary to domestic production. Of the dutiable imports, barely 8 per cent was substantially competitive. During 1933-6 restrictive action—mainly in the form of tariff increases—was taken against a number of these imports, including such items as canned fish, cotton, rugs, wool knit gloves, and rubber footwear.

The most serious agitation had arisen over imports of Japanese cotton cloth, which rose from 7,287,017 square yards in 1934 to 36,474,834 in 1935, valued respectively at $363,043 and $1,727,852. These imports constituted a negligible fraction of total domestic production, but were mainly concentrated in a special cloth which competed at a low price with the American

UNITED STATES IMPORTS FROM JAPAN IN 1934*

(of items valued at $12,000 or more, classified according to competitiveness)

Classification	*Value*	*Per Cent of Total Imports from Japan*
Total imports from Japan	$117,963,573	100.0
Imports of 271 items valued at $12,000 or more	116,391,752	98.7
I. Commodities imported free of duty	83,863,209	71.1
II. Dutiable imports	32,528,543	27.6
A. Commodities of which there is no domestic production	38,528,743	5.6
B. Commodities, the domestic production of which is insufficient	3,924,498	3.3
C. Commodities imported due to special conditions, either temporary or permanent, and not competitive at time or place of sale	363,726	0.3
D. Commodities of a type not produced in the United States, consumed mainly by Orientals	1,059,898	0.9
E. Commodities sold in the United States chiefly on the basis of their Oriental or novelty nature	3,437,687	2.9
F. Commodities distinctly different in type or grade from those produced in the United States	5,013,197	4.2
G. Commodities which are competitive but imports of which are negligible in comparison with domestic production	2,359,038	2.0
H. Commodities which are substantially competitive	9,713,756	8.2

* Compiled from *Recent Developments in the Foreign Trade of Japan* (Washington, United States Tariff Commission, 1936), Report No. 105, Second Series; for more detailed analysis, see "Japan's Trade Boom," *Foreign Policy Reports*, March 15, 1936.

product. In this range, for 1935, competition roughly centered on 30 million square yards of imported cloth as against domestic production of 150 million square yards, or 20 per cent of the total. A report issued on August 20, 1935 by a special Cabinet Committee, previously appointed by the President to investigate conditions in the cotton textile industry, recommended negotiation of an informal quota agreement with Japanese manufacturers covering textile products which had been the subject of complaint. Voluntary limitations imposed later by the Japanese industry were only partially effective, but toward the end of 1936 a comprehensive quota agreement was successfully concluded between the Japanese and American manufacturers. Following this agreement, which has been subsequently renewed, the phase of acute friction rapidly passed.

The second issue—competition in world markets—was also raised in sharpest form during the 1934-6 period, when the American trade recovery was proceeding much more slowly than Japan's phenomenal expansion. Effective competition, however, was limited in respect to both area and commodity. After 1929 the largest American trade losses were in Canada and in Europe, where Japanese competition was negligible. Even in Latin America where, for a brief period, Japan registered some of its most startling percentage increases, the absolute gains were small and remained only a fraction of American totals. After 1934, moreover, growing trade restrictions by Latin American countries limited Japan's further gains.[1] The greatest change was effected in the two countries' trade with the Netherlands Indies. In 1929 the United States accounted for 11.8 per cent of Netherlands Indies' imports, and Japan for 10.4 per cent; in 1934, these percentages had become, respectively, 6.0 and 31.6. In the Philippines, during the same period, American imports had increased from 62.9 to 65.4 per cent of the total, and Japanese imports from 8.1 to 12.4 per cent.

Severe competition was restricted to a few commodities, notably cotton cloth. Exports of American cotton cloth declined from an average of 540 million square yards in 1925-7 to 302 million square yards in 1933, 226 million in 1934, and 187 million in 1935. The declines in these latter years, despite the existence of other factors, were perhaps mainly the result of Japanese competition. Japan's exports of cotton cloth to the Philippines expanded rapidly after 1932, leading to decreased imports from the United States. On October 11, 1935 an agreement for voluntary limitation of Japan's exports of cotton cloth to the Philippines was concluded. The Japanese manufacturers agreed to limit exports to 45 million square meters annually for

[1] For this issue, and on the subject in general, see William W. Lockwood, *Trade and Trade Rivalry between the United States and Japan,* American Council, Institute of Pacific Relations, 1936.

a two-year period beginning August 1, 1935, provided the Philippine authorities levied no increase in the tariff duty on this commodity.[2] Although American producers were not wholly satisfied at the time, the agreement has worked satisfactorily. In the sphere of external trade competition, as well as in the American domestic market, Japanese-American friction lessened materially after 1935-6.

[2] State Department, *Press Releases,* October 19, 1935, pp. 309-11.

CHAPTER VI

THE PHILIPPINE COMMONWEALTH

During the years when Far Eastern stability was being rapidly undermined, fundamental changes were taking place in the relationship of the United States to the Philippine Islands. The strong movement for Philippine independence which developed in the United States after 1929 achieved its objectives in Congress at a time when the Manchurian dispute was at its height. In addition to those Congressional representatives who favored freedom for the Philippines on principle, the movement was supported by elements desiring to restrict immigration of Filipino laborers and imports of Philippine sugar, coconut oil and cordage. The original Hare-Hawes-Cutting Act was passed by Congress late in 1932, and then repassed over President Hoover's veto on January 17, 1933. It mustered little popular support, and public opinion in the country at large was apathetic. In October 1933, after a bitter political struggle in the Islands, the Philippine Legislature rejected the Act and passed a resolution in the following terms:

"That the Philippine Legislature, in its own name and in that of the Filipino people, inform the Congress of the United States that it declines to accept the said law in its present form because, in the opinion of the Legislature, among other reasons, the provisions of the law affecting trade relations between the United States and the Philippine Islands would seriously imperil the economic, social and political institutions of the country and might defeat its avowed purpose to secure independence to the Philippine Islands at the end of the transition period; because the immigration clause is objectionable and offensive to the Filipino people; because the powers of the High Commissioner are too indefinite; and finally because the military, naval and other reservations provided for in the said Act are inconsistent with true independence, violate national dignity and are subject to misunderstanding."[1]

[1] Ninth Philippine Legislature, 3rd. session, H. Ct. R., No. 61.

Early in 1934 a new Philippine independence bill was submitted to Congress. It embodied several changes, including provisions for surrender of American military reservations, for negotiations after independence as to disposition of the naval reservations, and for a trade conference one year prior to independence. Even in this form the Tydings-McDuffie Act, as approved March 24, 1934, did not essentially differ from the original law. When recommending the measure to Congress on March 2, 1934, President Roosevelt had declared: "I do not believe that further provisions of the original law need to be changed at this time. Where imperfections or inequalities exist, I am confident that both can be corrected after proper hearing and in fairness to both peoples." The Philippine Legislature, in accepting the new proposals on May 1, 1934, specifically referred to this Presidential pledge, as affording "reasonable assurance of further hearing and due consideration of their views."[2]

In accordance with the terms of the Independence Act, the following steps were thereupon taken:

(1) In July 1934 a constitutional convention of elected delegates assembled at Manila. The convention completed the drafting of a constitution on February 8, 1935.

(2) President Roosevelt, on March 23, 1935, certified this constitution as conforming substantially with the provisions of the Independence Act.

(3) The constitution was ratified by a plebiscite of the Philippine people on May 14, 1935.

(4) First elections of the Commonwealth of the Philippines were held on September 17, 1935. By large majorities, Manuel L. Quezon was elected President and Sergio Osmena, Vice-President.

(5) On November 15, 1935 the new Commonwealth government was formally inaugurated at Manila.

The constitution of the Philippine Commonwealth provided for a unicameral National Assembly of not more than 120 members, elected triennially. The President and Vice-President are elected by direct popular vote for a term of six years. While broadly autonomous in internal affairs, this Commonwealth government is restricted by important reservations of authority

[2] *Compilation of Documents Relating to the Inauguration of the Government of the Commonwealth of the Philippines,* 74th Congress, 2d session, House Document No. 400, p. 1.

to the United States.[3] Pending attainment of independence on July 4, 1946, Philippine citizens owe, and Philippine officials subscribe, allegiance to the United States. The United States retains direct supervision and control of Philippine foreign affairs, fixes the limits of the Philippine public debt, exerts the power of judicial review over court decisions, may intervene to preserve the Commonwealth government, and may call Philippine military forces into the service of American armed forces maintained in the Islands. Legislative acts must be reported to Congress, and the President must approve acts affecting currency, coinage, imports, exports, and immigration. The authority of an American High Commissioner, who possesses broad but undefined powers, must be recognized; the Commonwealth may also be represented by a Resident Commissioner at Washington.

These various limitations on full sovereignty are applicable during the Commonwealth period; after July 4, 1946, the independent Republic of the Philippines will come into existence. Two provisions in the original Hare-Hawes-Cutting Act to which the Philippine authorities took especial objection were not changed by the Independence Act. These involved, first, the "indefinite" powers of the High Commissioner; and, second, the substitution for free immigration of an annual quota of fifty immigrants prior to independence, with complete exclusion thereafter. Concessions to the Philippine viewpoint were made in the sphere of defense. The American military and naval reservations in the Islands are retained during the Commonwealth period. When the Republic is inaugurated, however, the military reservations will be surrendered, while naval reservations and fueling stations will be retained pending the results of negotiations as to their disposition which must begin within two years after independence.

While the extensive powers retained by the American Government during the transitional decade from 1936 to 1946, and more particularly the illiberal immigration provision may be subject to dispute, they are not determining factors in the outcome of the Philippine independence project. The ability of the new Philippine regime to establish and maintain an independent republic rests ultimately on two factors: successful

[3] Philippine Independence Act (Public, No. 127, 73d Cong.); for text of the Philippine Constitution, see *Compilation of Documents*, etc., cited, pp. 5-22.

readjustment of its economy to the loss of trade preference in the American market, and freedom from external aggression.

The political factor, viewed in the light of present conditions in the Far East, is a consideration of basic importance. Within the past year Japan's successive occupation of Canton, Hainan, and the Spratly Islands has increased the apprehension which has been developing in the Philippines, and has stimulated concern in the Islands lest they be cast adrift only to fall under Japanese domination. Despite the serious effort now being made to put the Philippine defense forces on an adequate footing, there is no certainty that these forces could of themselves successfully withstand attack by a major power. The problem of reconciling full Philippine autonomy with an assurance that the Islands will not be deprived of American support, when that support may prove vital to the maintenance of national freedom, is not an easy one to solve. Until 1946, at least, the issue does not arise in its most critical form; during the intervening period, the responsibility of the United States for preserving the Islands' integrity will still exist.

Decisions made in the interim on questions of Philippine-American economic relationships may prove equally decisive for the future stability of the Philippine Republic. The effects of the free trade regime, which has continuously existed between the United States and its Far Eastern dependency since 1909, cannot be substantially overcome within a brief period. During the 1928-37 decade, the Philippines sent between 75 and 87 per cent of its total annual exports to the United States, and obtained between 59 and 65 per cent of its annual imports in the American market.[4] In 1937 Philippine exports to the United States, valued at $122,755,000, constituted 80 per cent of its total exports; for 1936 the corresponding figures were $107,534,000, and 79 per cent. An abrupt severance of its ties with the American market would have a disastrous reaction on the Philippine economy. For the United States, which sent but 2.5 per cent of its total 1936 exports to the Philippines, discontinuance of the preferential free-trade relationship is comparatively unimportant.

Detailed commodity trade figures bring out even more clearly the extent of Philippine economic dependence on the United

[4] Trade figures cited in this paper are taken from *Report of the Joint Preparatory Committee on Philippine Affairs*, Washington, 1938, Vol. I.

States. Sugar alone accounted for $57,611,000, or 47 per cent, of total Philippine exports to the United States in 1937; and for $61,927,000, or 58 per cent, in 1936. The percentages of other leading Philippine exports taken by the United States in 1937 are as follows: abaca or manila hemp (32), coconut oil (98), copra (90), desiccated coconut (99), tobacco and products (66), timber and lumber (32), embroideries (99), copra cake and meal (49), canned pineapples (100), and cordage (35). Not all of these exports were dependent on trade preference. In the dependent class should be placed sugar, coconut oil, tobacco products, cordage, embroideries, and pearl buttons. On the other hand, copra, abaca, leaf tobacco and timber are sold at world prices, either in the United States or elsewhere, and large land acreages are devoted to crops of rice, corn and sweet potatoes which are consumed domestically. Even with these qualifications, the necessity of cushioning the shock of too abrupt a transition is obvious.

This necessity was ostensibly reckoned with in the trade provisions of the Independence Act. Four main planks are laid down in the economic sections of the act, as follows:

(1) During the Commonwealth period, the annual duty-free quota of sugar is fixed at 850,000 long tons, of coconut oil at 200,000 long tons, and of cordage at 3,000,000 pounds; excess exports of these commodities pay the full American duty.

(2) Beginning on November 15, 1940, the Philippine government is directed to levy an export tax of 5 per cent of the American tariff rate on all Philippine commodities, including those subjected to quota limitations, entering the United States duty-free. Each year thereafter the export tax shall be increased by an additional 5 per cent until it reaches 25 per cent of the American tariff rates during the last year of the Commonwealth. Revenues thus derived must be applied to the liquidation of the bonded indebtedness of the Philippine Islands, national and local.

(3) In 1946, after independence is attained, Philippine products are to be assessed the full United States customs duties.

(4) A Philippines-United States trade conference shall be held at least one year prior to independence for the purpose of formulating recommendations as to future trade relationships.

The essential elements in this program were wholly lacking in reciprocity. The Philippine government has no authority to curtail American imports into the Islands, nor to alter Philippine tariff rates except by consent of the President. Certain modifications subsequently enacted by Congress, moreover, tended to increase the inequity of the trade provisions of the Independence Act.[5]

Under these conditions, and particularly in view of the President's statement to the effect that such "imperfections and inequalities" as existed in the Independence Act should be corrected, steps to remove objections to the act were initiated even before the inauguration of the Commonwealth government. In 1934 several Senators, after visits to the Philippines, submitted reports to the Senate.[6] At the end of 1934 an Interdepartmental Committee on Philippine Affairs, in which representatives of the Departments of State, War, Navy, Treasury, Agriculture and Commerce, and of the Tariff Commission, have participated, was organized to direct studies and co-ordinate administrative activities concerned with Philippine affairs. On April 10, 1935, on recommendation of the Interdepartmental Committee, President Roosevelt announced his intention of calling the joint trade conference provided for in the Independence Act as soon as practicable. Two years later, after trade studies had been prepared both by the United States Tariff Commission and by a Committee in the Philippines, the Joint Preparatory Committee on Philippine Affairs was established to complete these studies and recommend a program for the adjustment of the Philippine national economy. This Committee, under the chairmanship of Mr. J. V. A. MacMurray, was composed of six Philippine and six American members. As the study of the Joint Preparatory Committee progressed, the need for extending the period of Philippine trade adjustment to 1960 became apparent. This proposal was approved in an exchange of telegrams be-

[5] The quotas on sugar and cordage (this latter, however, at a higher figure) were changed from a "duty-free" to an "absolute" basis, and an American excise tax was levied on coconut oil imports. American excises are also levied on sugar and cigars coming from the Philippines. The proceeds of these excise taxes are remitted to the Philippine Treasury. On the other hand, it should be noted that while the Philippine Commonwealth levies excise taxes on certain American products, such as cigarettes, liquors and kerosene, it retains the proceeds of such taxes for its own use.

[6] Including a report by Senator Carl Hayden; also two reports from a special committee, consisting of Senators Tydings, McKellar, McAdoo and Gibson, appointed on June 16, 1934 to investigate the "imperfections or inequalities" of the Independence Act.

tween President Roosevelt and President Quezon in March 1938, the substance of which was as follows:

"On March 22, President Roosevelt telegraphed to President Quezon an expression of his feeling that the work of the [Joint Preparatory] Committee should be pressed to an early and mutually satisfactory conclusion. The President recalled that he had already made publicly known his own readiness, with a view to affording the Philippines ample opportunity to adjust their economy to the non-preferential status of political independence, to approve of a general plan by which the elimination of trade preferences would proceed by uniform annual accretions of 5 per cent, from 25 per cent at the date of independence; but he indicated that, except for certain alleviations which he understood the Committee would be prepared to recommend, the export tax provisions of the Independence Act should remain substantially intact as constituting a necessary part of the program of Philippine economic adjustment. The President furthermore suggested that President Quezon join with him in making public their common desire to have the Committee proceed along these lines with a view to reaching an early agreement upon recommendations which would have the wholehearted support of both sides.

"In a telegram dated March 25, President Quezon replied that he was sending to the Filipino members of the Joint Preparatory Committee a radiogram to the effect that he had, after considering all the attending circumstances, come to the definite conclusion that the best interests of the Philippines would be promoted by their concurring with the American members of the Committee in the plan outlined in the President's telegram."[7]

Following this exchange of telegrams between President Roosevelt and President Quezon, the Joint Preparatory Committee rapidly completed the preparation of its report, which was published on May 20, 1938. It found that, under the trade provisions of the Independence Act, "a number of important enterprises in the Philippines will be forced to liquidate much more rapidly than new enterprises can probably be developed to replace them."[8] Exports of coconut oil, cigars and other to-

[7] State Department, *Press Releases,* April 9, 1938, pp. 464-5.
[8] Vol. I, p. 22.

bacco products, embroideries, and pearl buttons, according to "reasonably certain" expectations, would be sharply curtailed or cut off entirely after 1946, while substantial reductions might be caused before then by the export taxes. In the case of sugar, the export taxes would "serve primarily to lessen the profitableness, but not the volume" of exports during the Commonwealth period; after 1946, when the full United States tariff duties became applicable, the position of the sugar industry was "largely indeterminate," although its future, on the basis of current prices, "does not appear promising." Various other Philippine products would probably be less seriously affected, provided no changes were made in the American tariff schedule then prevailing.

In line with these judgments, the Committee recommended that "trade preferences should not be terminated on July 4, 1946, but should, by a process of gradual elimination, be terminated at the end of the year 1960."[9] The Committee suggested retention of the Independence Act provision for graduated export taxes rising to 25 per cent in 1946 on Philippine products entering the United States. After 1946, however, instead of an application of full tariff rates, the Committee recommended that the same progression of 5 per cent annual increases be continued in the form of import taxes levied both on Philippine products entering the United States and American products entering the Philippines. Thus, beginning with 25 per cent of prevailing American and Philippine tariff rates in 1946, these duties would be mutually raised by 5 per cent each year until January 1, 1961, when full duties would be assessed by both countries.

Under the terms of this recommendation, progressive Philippine export taxes would be maintained until 1946 on duty-free quotas for sugar (850,000 long tons) and cordage (6,000,000 pounds after May 1, 1941). After 1946 the quotas on these products would be retained, subject to graduated United States import duties, beginning at 25 per cent and rising 5 per cent annually until 1961. The Committee also recommended special treatment for cigars, certain tobacco products, coconut oil, and pearl buttons—the commodities which would have been most seriously affected by the export taxes. For these products the Committee suggested a series of annually declining duty-free quotas, instead of progressively increasing export taxes, for the

[9] For the Committee's recommendations, see Vol. I, pp. 35-7; 161-73.

1940-6 period; and similar quotas, declining in still greater proportion, for the period from 1946 to 1960. The Committee also recommended that a Philippine-American commercial treaty be "negotiated at the earliest practicable date, in order that the future trade relationship between the two countries may be definitely determined well in advance of independence."[10]

The Committee expressed the opinion that, if the trade programs thus recommended were carried out, the Philippines would be afforded "a reasonable opportunity to adjust its economy to a non-preferential basis."[11] In order to attain this objective, however, the Philippine government would have to adopt and carry through a long-range program of economic readjustment. Extensive suggestions for such a program, including projects dealing with technical training, agriculture, manufacturing, transportation, tariff schedules (virtually unchanged for 30 years), public revenue systems, and health conditions, are contained in the Committee's report.[12] This program should be "designed as an entirety" and therefore should be formulated by an organization of trained technicians—adequately staffed, completely non-administrative in character, and on at least a semi-permanent basis. Finally, the Committee suggested that the proceeds of United States excise taxes on Philippine sugar and coconut products should be set aside for the financing of the economic adjustment program.

In order to effectuate the Committee's recommendations, certain amendments to the Independence Act had to be passed by Congress.[13] The items in the Joint Committee's suggested program for trade revision were substantially incorporated in a bill introduced by Senator Tydings which was referred to the Insular and Territories Committee of the Senate.[14] Opposition by certain Committee members, notably on the issue of deferring application of full tariffs until 1961, threatened for a time to block consideration of the bill. A compromise "minimum," which the Administration worked out in conference with the

[10] Vol. I, p. 173.
[11] *Ibid.*, p. 127.
[12] *Ibid.*, pp. 127-49.
[13] For details of amendments passed by the regular session of Congress in 1939, see Frederick T. Merrill, "The Outlook for Philippine Independence," *Foreign Policy Reports,* September 15, 1939, pp. 156-8.
[14] S. 1028, 76th Congress, 1st Session.

Committee leaders, was eventually passed by the Senate on May 31, 1939. The bill prepared by the House of Representatives, however, owing to the latter's priority rights in the initiation of revenue legislation, became the measure finally approved by Congress.[15] The agricultural lobbies centered their attention on this House bill and succeeded in effecting a number of modifications which suited their interests. Passed by Congress on July 31 and signed by the President on August 7, the measure enters into effect after approval by the Philippine Commonwealth.

The Congressional amendments to the Independence Act thus adopted depart widely from the liberal recommendations of the Joint Preparatory Committee. Its basic contention that the period for adjustment of the Philippine economy should be extended fifteen years to 1961 was set aside. The new amendments, which are limited to the period up to July 3, 1946, ignore the Joint Committee's proposals for tariff increases on a progressive scale after that date. Full American tariff rates will therefore be applied to Philippine exports to the United States after July 1946.

Most of the other recommendations of the Joint Committee, however, were incorporated in the amendments passed by Congress. The annually declining duty-free quotas suggested by the Committee for several Philippine export products were made effective, but only for the 1940-6 period. The original quotas, effective beginning January 1, 1940, are set for these products at the following levels: cigars (200,000,000), scrap tobacco (4,500,000 pounds), coconut oil (200,000 long tons), and pearl or shell buttons (850,000 gross). Each year thereafter, in lieu of the export tax, these quotas will be reduced by 5 per cent; full American tariffs will be levied after July 1946 without benefit of duty-free quotas.[16] Copra and manila (abaca) fiber were relieved from imposition of the progressive export tax. In computing the export tax on Philippine embroideries, an allowance is to be deducted from the taxable value equal to the cost, insurance and freight of any cloth of American origin used in the process of production. On all other Philippine products, including sugar, the progressive export tax, increasing at the rate of 5 per cent annually, shall be levied between January 1, 1941 and July 3,

[15] H. R. 7096, 76th Congress, 1st Session.
[16] H. R. 7096, Sec. 6 (b) (3).

1946.[17] For this period the annual quota of Philippine sugar, admitted to the United States free of duty, was fixed at 850,000 long tons, of which not more than 50,000 long tons may be refined sugar. The Philippine cordage quota was continued at 6 million pounds annually until July 3, 1946.

These amendments to the Independence Act will help to stabilize the Philippine economic situation until July 1946. After that date, however, the imposition of full American duties will exert serious effects on the Philippine economy. The cigar, scrap tobacco, embroidery, and pearl button industries can hardly be expected to survive. In the case of sugar, only the most efficient Philippine producers would be able to compete successfully in a free market. A partial continuance, at least, of existing tariff and quota preferences appears necessary in order to maintain the Philippine sugar industry at its present level. The coconut oil industry, second in importance to sugar in Philippine export trade, is threatened by the growth of American excise and intrastate protective taxes, which are vigorously supported by American dairy and farm groups.[18] It is still possible that further adjustments in Philippine-American trade relations may be effected before July 1946. The 1939 amendments to the Independence Act advanced by one year, i.e., to 1944, the date for a trade conference of Philippine-American government representatives. This conference may afford the final opportunity to reach commercial adjustments which will assure the stability of Philippine economy after independence.

During its first four years, the Philippine Commonwealth has made an encouraging start in dealing with its social, economic and political problems.[19] Minimum wage laws and the eight-hour day are being extended, the newly established Labor Relations Board has facilitated collective bargaining, efforts toward resettlement of large estates and introduction of co-operative farming and marketing have been made, political prisoners have been amnestied, and improvements in the civil service, state

[17] For the final half year, January 1 to July 3, 1946, the rate will remain 25 per cent.

[18] For additional details on the outlook for Philippine sugar and coconut oil, see Frederick T. Merrill, "The Outlook for Philippine Independence," cited pp. 158-9.

[19] David H. Popper, "Creating a Philippine Commonwealth," *Foreign Policy Reports,* December 15, 1936; James S. Allen, "Democracy and Independence in the Philippines," *Amerasia,* March 1939; Federico Mangahas, "Current Political Journalism in the Philippines," *Amerasia,* September 1939.

finances, and the judiciary launched. On the whole, these and other measures still constitute but a beginning in the fields represented; nevertheless, they indicate a significant trend in the direction of soundly conceived democratic reform. The eventual outcome of the Philippine experiment in self-government depends largely on the economic relationship worked out with the United States and the re-establishment of stability and peace in the Far East.

CHAPTER VII

THE SINO-JAPANESE WAR, 1937-1939

A deceptive calm prevailed in the Far East during the early months of 1937. Four years had passed since the first phase of the Sino-Japanese conflict had culminated on the one hand in the League Assembly's adoption of its Manchurian report, and on the other in the Tangku Truce. During these years the political aspects of the continued Japanese penetration of China aroused relatively slight interest in the West. The flurries created by the Amau statement and the "autonomy movement" in North China were of brief duration. In the United States, equal or greater attention was devoted to naval issues, Japanese trade competition, and the establishment of the Philippine Commonwealth. Few observers, in the spring of 1937, would have dared to predict that the third, and most serious, phase of the contemporary Far Eastern crisis was imminent.

Two months before the Lukouchiao incident of July 7, 1937, the American Congress had passed a revised and strengthened Neutrality Act. This Act, as well as its predecessors, constituted evidence of the strong isolationist sentiment which had developed in the United States after 1935. At the outset of the Manchurian dispute, the American people had largely supported the measures taken by the State Department in co-operation with the League of Nations. Faith in the possibilities of international action to curb aggression was still active. Such feelings reached their climax during the Shanghai hostilities early in 1932, when American opinion was perhaps sufficiently aroused to have supported the application of sanctions against Japan. A year elapsed, however, before the Lytton Commission's report was approved by the League Assembly; in the interim, public feeling in the United States had markedly subsided, and there was little or no pressure to secure enforcement of the League's decision. Early hearings of the Senate Munitions Investigation Committee, published during 1934, cast a spotlight on the way in which the United States became involved in the World War and led to formation of a strong "neutrality bloc" in Congress.

When the Ethiopian dispute arose in 1935, and it was seen that the League of Nations had actually embarked on a program of sanctions against Italy, renewed demand for active American assistance to the League's policy was expressed in the United States. A *Fortune* survey during this period indicated that a majority of the American people was prepared to support economic sanctions against an aggressor.[1] The Hoare-Laval fiasco, and the eventual failure of the half-hearted sanctions imposed against Italy by the League, went far toward disillusioning the American public. Fear lest the United States become involved in war was intensified by the Ethiopian dispute, and on August 31, 1935 neutrality advocates in Congress secured passage of the first Neutrality Act. By joint resolution, Congress provided for an embargo on the export of implements of war to belligerents "upon the outbreak or during the progress of war," and gave the President discretion to prohibit Americans from traveling on belligerent vessels except at their own risk.[2] An extension of this act, effected February 9, 1936, reduced the President's discretion relative to imposition of the arms embargo, added an embargo on loans to belligerents, and exempted American republics from its provisions. Finally, on May 1, 1937, Congress passed a more elaborate act which made the arms embargo applicable whenever the President found that "a state of war" existed between foreign states, and whenever "a state of civil strife" likely to endanger the peace of the United States existed in a foreign state. In addition, the President was given discretionary authority to place other commodities on a "cash-and-carry" basis, thus limiting transport of such commodities to foreign vessels after ownership had been transferred to the belligerent state or its representatives.[3]

The successive implementations of this neutrality legislation reflected a strong current of isolationist feeling among the American people, taking the form of an attempt to insulate the United States from the growing political unsettlement in Eu-

[1] Cited by Miriam Farley, *American Far Eastern Policy and the Sino-Japanese War*, American Council, Institute of Pacific Relations, p. 52.

[2] For detailed analysis, see R. L. Buell, "The New American Neutrality," *Foreign Policy Reports*, January 15, 1936.

[3] For text of resolution, and analysis of its provisions, see R. L. Buell, "The Neutrality Act of 1937," *Foreign Policy Reports*, October 1, 1937.

rope.[4] Congressional sponsors of the legislation had made little real effort to appraise possible effects in the Far East, where the activities of Japan, an industrialized power controlling the seas but in need of American materials, ran counter to the interests, policy and sentiment of the United States. The Lukouchiao incident again brought the United States face to face with the Far Eastern issue, which had virtually lain dormant since 1933. After the spread of Sino-Japanese hostilities from North China to Shanghai, the problem of determining the American official attitude toward the dispute became pressing. In the early stages of the conflict, decisions revolved mainly about the methods to be adopted for protection of American nationals in China and the desirability of invoking the provisions of the Neutrality Act. Underlying these immediate issues was the basic question of whether the United States could "stay out of war" by pursuing the isolationist policy implicit in the neutrality legislation or by co-operating where feasible with other nations to halt aggression and prevent the outbreak of general war. This basic question became steadily more acute with the progress of Sino-Japanese hostilities and the increasing threat of war in Europe. Through 1938 and 1939 it was debated by an ever larger proportion of the American public—and the course of this debate was reflected in official American policy toward the Far Eastern conflict.

From Lukouchiao to the Panay Incident

During the sporadic clashes near Peiping in July 1937, Secretary Hull sought cautiously to define the general principles of the American position, along with mild overtures toward international support. As early as July 12 the State Department informed the Japanese Ambassador and the Counselor of the Chinese Embassy that the American government would regard "an armed conflict" as "a great blow to the cause of peace and world progress."[5] Four days later the Secretary of State issued a carefully formulated declaration of American policy. While not re-

[4] Early polls by the Gallup Institute, issued on November 17, 1935, revealed the general hold neutrality sentiment had already acquired. One showed 71 per cent opposing, and 29 per cent favoring, joint action with other nations to enforce peace; another showed 47 per cent favoring prohibition of all trade with belligerents, 37 per cent willing to sell war materials only, and 16 per cent desiring no restrictions on trade.

[5] State Department, *Press Releases,* July 17, 1937, p. 31.

ferring specifically to either China or Japan, it was obviously intended as a warning to the latter. The American government, in this statement of July 16, expressed its adherence to the following set of international principles:

"This country constantly and consistently advocates maintenance of peace. We advocate national and international self-restraint. We advocate abstinence by all nations from use of force in pursuit of policy and from interference in the internal affairs of other nations. We advocate adjustment of problems in international relations by processes of peaceful negotiation and agreement. We advocate faithful observance of international agreements. Upholding the principle of the sanctity of treaties, we believe in modification of provisions of treaties, when need therefor arises, by orderly processes carried out in a spirit of mutual helpfulness and accommodation. We believe in respect by all nations for the rights of others and performance by all nations of established obligations. We stand for revitalizing and strengthening of international law. We advocate steps toward promotion of economic security and stability the world over. We advocate lowering or removing excessive barriers in international trade. We seek effective equality of commercial opportunity and we urge upon all nations application of the principle of equality of treatment. We believe in limitation and reduction of armament. Realizing the necessity for maintaining armed forces adequate for national security, we are prepared to reduce or to increase our own armed forces in proportion to reductions or increases made by other countries. We avoid entering into alliances or entangling commitments but we believe in cooperative effort by peaceful and practicable means in support of the principles hereinbefore stated."[6]

The preamble to this declaration of principles, containing the assertion that "any situation in which armed hostilities are in progress or are threatened" may seriously affect the rights and interests of all nations, might have been construed as an oblique reference to neutrality sentiment at home as well as to Japan's actions. The text of the statement was communicated to other governments; to this extent at least, Secretary Hull's effort was directed toward marshaling world opinion against the threat of war in the Orient. Replies were received from more than sixty nations. Except for Portugal, which vigorously attacked an at-

[6] *Ibid.*, p. 41-2.

tempt to solve grave problems by "vague formulae" in a lengthy communication,[7] nearly all states expressed approval. The Japanese government, while subscribing to the general principles of Secretary Hull's statement, made an important reservation by declaring that the objectives could "only be attained, in their application to the Far Eastern situation, by a full recognition and practical consideration of the actual particular circumstances of that region."[8]

Through August and most of September, sharp controversy was waged in the United States over two concrete issues: protection of American citizens in China, and invocation of the Neutrality Act. Several peace organizations and a number of isolationist Congressmen clamored for withdrawal of American civilians and armed forces from China.[9] In addition to the so-called Fifteenth Infantry (some 700 men) at Tientsin, the United States maintained a Marine Guard of 500 at Peiping and a force of 1,000 marines at Shanghai. On August 17, when announcement was made that 1,200 additional marines were being sent from San Diego to Shanghai, Secretary Hull declared that the State Department was pursuing a "middle-of-the-road" policy, neither abandoning American interests and nationals nor supporting them by excessively large military-naval forces.[10] The deaths of three Americans from bombs dropped on the Shanghai Settlement by Chinese fliers, and the ensuing attack on the *President Hoover* by a Chinese airman, led to reinforcement of previous official advices that Americans should withdraw from threatened areas. On September 3 urgent warnings were given to American citizens to leave Shanghai on waiting naval vessels. Two days later, at an informal press conference, President Roosevelt declared that Americans who chose to remain after repeated warnings did so at their own risk.[11] This statement called forth a flood of protests, including stiff cablegrams from the American Chambers of Commerce at Shanghai and Tientsin. Nevertheless, a considerable evacuation of Americans occurred, mainly from Shanghai. More than 3,000 Ameri-

[7] State Department, *Press Releases,* September 18, 1937, pp. 229-34.

[8] *Ibid.,* August 21, 1937, p. 130.

[9] For statements at this time by Congressional neutrality advocates, see Whitney H. Shepardson and William O. Scroggs, *The United States in World Affairs, 1937,* pp. 43-52.

[10] *New York Times,* August 18, 1937.

[11] *New York Times,* September 6, 1937.

cans had been evacuated by September 25, and over 4,500 by October 29, leaving approximately 5,800 in China.[12] Opinion in the United States at this time, while apparently favoring withdrawal of civilians, was divided on the issue of protection; a poll of the Gallup Institute, published on September 5, 1937, showed 54 per cent favoring withdrawal of American armed forces from China, with 46 per cent opposed.

An equally severe struggle raged over the propriety of invoking the Neutrality Act. On July 29 Senator Pittman, chairman of the Senate Foreign Relations Committee, issued a formal statement maintaining that every armed conflict was not a state of war, and arguing that the President's influence in protecting American citizens and bringing about a cessation of the conflict would be lessened by application of the neutrality statute. At this stage, editorial comment and popular opinion seemed to favor Senator Pittman's viewpoint.[13] After the initial events at Shanghai, attitude and opinion markedly changed. Senators Nye and Clark declared that the law should be applied, even though it might give Japan an advantage over China.[14] Twenty-four members of the House issued a joint statement urging that Congress remain in session long enough to take "every possible action to protect this country against becoming involved in the Far Eastern war."[15] Telegrams and letters, resolutions by peace societies, and open letters to the President subjected Congress and the Administration to heavy pressure.

Two spokesmen for the Administration, Senator Pittman and Secretary Hull, replied to the criticism on August 23. Speaking over the radio, Senator Pittman stressed the fact that neither China nor Japan had declared war, reiterated his contention that protection of American citizens would be rendered more difficult if the United States recognized a state of war by invoking the Neutrality Act, and stigmatized the clamor for withdrawal of American armed forces from the Far East as "cowardly and unpatriotic."[16] Secretary Hull stated that the American

[12] State Department, *Press Releases,* October 2, 1937, p. 267; November 6, p. 351.

[13] Shepardson and Scroggs, cited, pp. 200-1.

[14] *New York Times,* August 18, 1937. See also Senator Nye's statement that the issue of the partiality or impartiality of the law was irrelevant; its sole purpose "was to keep the country out of war." *Congressional Record,* 75th Cong., 1st session, p. 12371.

[15] *New York Times,* August 20, 1937.

[16] *Ibid.,* August 24, 1937.

government was facilitating "an orderly and safe removal of American citizens" from dangerous areas, while continuing "to afford its nationals appropriate protection." The government believed neither in "political alliances" nor in "extreme isolation;" it was "participating constantly in consultation with interested governments directed toward peaceful adjustment;" and was giving "solicitous attention to every phase of the Far Eastern situation" in an effort to make effective "the policies—especially the policy of peace—in which this country believes and to which it is committed."[17] While Secretary Hull's exposition of policy constituted an implied answer to critics of the State Department, his studied avoidance of any mention of the Neutrality Act itself—or of its probable application in the near future—was even more revelatory of the government's attitude toward the usefulness of that law in the Far Eastern conflict.

Strong public pressure for enforcement of the Neutrality Act continued during the rest of August and into September. Fresh fuel was added to the controversy on August 25, when the Japanese naval authorities declared a blockade of part of China's coastal area. At first some doubt existed as to whether the blockade applied to foreign as well as Chinese vessels; if the former, Japan was in effect claiming belligerent rights, and thus presenting a new argument to advocates of the need for invoking the Neutrality Act. This issue, moreover, arose at a moment when isolationist groups were spotlighting the passage of the *Wichita*, a government-owned vessel carrying 19 airplanes for China, from the east to the west coasts. Secretary Hull had already notified China and Japan that the American government reserved all rights on behalf of its nationals for damages growing out of the operations of their military forces. On September 10, however, he warned of dangers to shipping along the China coast, and on September 14 the President made the following announcement:

"Merchant vessels owned by the Government of the United States will not hereafter, until further notice, be permitted to transport to China or Japan any of the arms, ammunition, or implements of war which were listed in the President's proclamation of May 1, 1937.

"Any other merchant vessels, flying the American flag, which

[17] State Department, *Press Releases,* August 28, 1937, pp. 166-7.

attempt to transport any of the listed articles to China or Japan will, until further notice, do so at their own risk.

"The question of applying the Neutrality Act remains *in status quo*, the Government policy remaining on a 24-hour basis."[18]

As a sequel to this announcement, the *Wichita* unloaded the planes at San Pedro and proceeded to Manila and Hongkong with another cargo. The Chinese government registered a vain protest on September 17; after long delay, the planes were re-routed to China by way of Europe. Only four government-owned vessels were engaged in the Far Eastern trade, but the effects of the warning to private vessels were more significant, since they made "it difficult for the Chinese government to secure tonnage for shipment of arms across the Pacific."[19] As American shippers engaged in the carrying trade to Japan ran virtually no risk, the warning by the President applied unequally to the two belligerents. On the other hand, the President's action—which partially invoked one provision of the Neutrality Act—tended to pull the teeth of the isolationist opposition on a strategic issue. At this juncture, moreover, Japan's resort to unrestricted bombing stirred and angered foreign opinion, both in the United States and Europe; the demand for application of the neutrality statute lessened, and thereafter did not again reach the same proportions.

Extensive air raids on Nanking and other Chinese cities, occurring toward the end of September, caused widespread loss of civilian life and endangered the members of foreign embassies. Preliminary warnings from the Japanese naval commander urged foreign officials and residents to move up-river from Nanking "into areas of greater safety" before noon of September 21. The first raids on Nanking were actually made on September 19, and were repeated on the 22nd, 25th and 28th; during this period large civilian casualties, running into the thousands, were also reported from Canton and Hankow as the result of similar bombings. On September 22, after previous representations through diplomatic channels, Secretary Hull addressed a sharp protest to Japan.

"This Government," the note stated, "holds the view that

[18] State Department, *Press Releases*, September 18, 1937, p. 237.

[19] Paul B. Taylor, "America's Role in the Far Eastern Conflict," *Foreign Policy Reports*, February 15, 1938, p. 281.

any general bombing of an extensive area wherein there resides a large populace engaged in peaceful pursuits is unwarranted and contrary to principles of law and of humanity. Moreover, in the present instance the period allowed for withdrawal is inadequate, and, in view of the wide area over which Japanese bombing operations have prevailed, there can be no assurance that even in areas to which American nationals and noncombatants might withdraw they would be secure. . . .

"In view of the fact that Nanking is the seat of government in China and that there the American Ambassador and other agencies of the American Government carry on their essential functions, the American Government strongly objects to the creation of a situation in consequence of which the American Ambassador and other agencies of this Government are confronted with the alternative of abandoning their establishments or being exposed to grave hazards.

"The American Government, therefore, reserving all rights on its own behalf and on behalf of American nationals in respect to damages which might result from Japanese military operations in the Nanking area, expresses the earnest hope that further bombing in and around the city of Nanking will be avoided."[20]

Strong protests were made by Great Britain and France; Germany and Italy made representations at Tokyo; and the Soviet Union served notice that it would hold Japan responsible for any damages to its Embassy at Nanking. At Geneva, on September 28, the League Assembly unanimously approved a resolution expressing its "profound distress at the loss of life caused to innocent civilians, including great numbers of women and children," and declared that "no excuse can be made for such acts, which have aroused horror and indignation throughout the world."[21] Foreign Minister Hirota's early informal replies to these protests stated that no attacks would be made on noncombatants, and indicated that the warnings had been motivated by a desire to ensure the safety of foreigners. His formal reply of September 29 to the American note, however, bluntly rejected every point raised by the American government and strictly defended the Japanese actions. The bombing of Nanking, the reply asserted, was "a necessary and unavoidable

[20] State Department, *Press Releases,* September 25, 1937, pp. 255-6.
[21] League of Nations, *Official Journal,* Special Supplement, No. 177.

measure for the attainment of the military objectives of the Japanese forces." The "rights and interests of third countries and the safety of the lives and property of the nationals thereof" would be respected "as far as possible," but injury "might be unavoidable notwithstanding the greatest precautions which may be taken by the Japanese forces." The Japanese government adhered to its previously stated position of recognizing no responsibility "with regard to damages sustained by nationals of third countries as a result of the present hostilities in China."[22]

One week later, President Roosevelt delivered an address at Chicago which vigorously attacked the isolationist position and strongly affirmed the necessity of international action in restraint of aggression.

"The peace-loving nations," the President declared, "must make a concerted effort in opposition to those violations of treaties and those ignorings of humane instincts which today are creating a state of international anarchy and instability from which there is no escape through mere isolation or neutrality. . . .

"There is a solidarity and interdependence about the modern world, both technically and morally, which makes it impossible for any nation completely to isolate itself from economic and political upheavals in the rest of the world, especially when such upheavals appear to be spreading and not declining. There can be no stability or peace either within nations or between nations except under laws and moral standards adhered to by all. International anarchy destroys every foundation for peace. It jeopardizes either the immediate or the future security of every nation, large or small. It is, therefore, a matter of vital interest and concern to the people of the United States that the sanctity of international treaties and the maintenance of international morality be restored. . . .

"It seems to be unfortunately true that the epidemic of world lawlessness is spreading. When an epidemic of physical disease starts to spread, the community approves and joins in a quarantine of the patients in order to protect the health of the community against the spread of the disease. . . .

"War is a contagion, whether it be declared or undeclared. It can engulf states and peoples remote from the original scene of

[22] State Department, *Press Releases,* October 2, 1937, pp. 268-9.

the hostilities. We are determined to keep out of war, yet we cannot insure ourselves against the disastrous effects of war and the dangers of involvement. We are adopting such measures as will minimize our risk of involvement, but we cannot have complete protection in a world of disorder in which confidence and security have broken down. . . .

"Most important of all, the will for peace on the part of peace-loving nations must express itself to the end that nations that may be tempted to violate their agreements and the rights of others will desist from such a course. There must be positive endeavors to preserve peace."[23]

This vigorous statement was made on October 5, the day on which the League's Far Eastern Advisory Committee, with a non-voting American delegate participating, adopted two reports and laid them before the League Assembly.[24] In its first report, the Committee concluded that Japan's military operations were "out of all proportion to the incident that occasioned the conflict," that neither "existing legal instruments" nor "the right of self-defense" constituted adequate justification for these operations, and that they contravened Japan's obligations under the Nine-Power Treaty and the Pact of Paris. The Committee's second report suggested that the states most interested in the Far East should be brought together "to seek a method of putting an end to the conflict by agreement." The Assembly should therefore request League members, who were signatories of the Nine-Power Treaty, to initiate consultation provided for in that treaty and invite other interested states to associate with them in their task. On October 6 the Assembly adopted these reports, with but two states—Siam and Poland—abstaining.

At Washington, on the same day, Secretary Hull aligned the United States with these decisions of the League. After briefly recapitulating the American position toward the Sino-Japanese conflict, he concluded with these words:

"In the light of the unfolding developments in the Far East, the government of the United States has been forced to the conclusion that the action of Japan in China is inconsistent with the principles which should govern the relationships between nations and is contrary to the provisions of the Nine-Power Treaty of February 6, 1922, regarding principles and policies to

[23] State Department, *Press Releases,* October 9, 1937, pp. 275-9.

[24] League of Nations, *Official Journal,* Special Supplement, No. 177, pp. 37-44.

be followed in matters concerning China, and to those of the Kellogg-Briand Pact of August 27, 1928. Thus the conclusions of this Government with respect to the foregoing are in general accord with those of the Assembly of the League of Nations."[25]

The immediate reaction of the American public to President Roosevelt's speech and the League Assembly's initiative was divided. Advocates of international measures to restrain aggression were heartened by these events. The boycott of Japanese goods received a strong impetus in the United States, and was taken up in other countries. A closely reasoned statement by Mr. Stimson in support of an embargo on American economic supplies to Japan, appearing in the *New York Times* for October 7, undoubtedly expressed the feeling of many Americans. On the other hand, the word "quarantine" seems to have generated uneasiness and fear among wide groups of the population that shunned anything smacking of "involvement" by the United States in the Far Eastern conflict. Congress was not in session, but appeals from constituents received by Congressmen evidently reflected a strong negative reaction to adoption of positive measures against Japan.[26] The Philadelphia *Inquirer* conducted a telegraphic poll of Congressional representatives; the majority against common action with the League along sanctionist lines was more than two to one.[27]

As preparations for the meeting to be held under the Nine-Power Treaty went forward, the Administration took pains to emphasize that the purpose of the conference was to seek a solution "by agreement."[28] The American delegates to the Brussels Conference were Mr. Norman Davis, assisted by Dr. Stanley K. Hornbeck and Mr. Pierrepont Moffat as technical advisers. Before the delegation sailed, statements both at Washington and London indicated that there was small likelihood of the adoption of a sanctionist program at Brussels. The conference assembled on November 3, with nineteen countries represented. Ignoring a plea for firm action from M. Litvinov, the Soviet delegate, the conference restricted itself to efforts at mediation and conciliation. When Japan refused to accept a twice-repeated invitation to attend the conference, the work of the delegates

[25] State Department, *Press Releases,* October 9, 1937, p. 310.

[26] Shephardson and Scroggs, cited, p. 222.

[27] *New York Times,* October 9, 1937.

[28] This statement was made by President Roosevelt in a radio talk on October 12, 1937.

was brought to a standstill. On November 24, after issuing a declaration of principles and a report of its activities, the conference adjourned—although not without an assertion of its intention to reconvene when the possibility of effective action should emerge.[29]

On December 12, less than three weeks later, the American gunboat *Panay* was bombed and sunk by Japanese airplanes at a point some twenty miles above Nanking on the Yangtze River. Two members of the crew lost their lives, several were severely wounded and an Italian correspondent on board the *Panay* later succumbed to his wounds; a captain of one of the three Standard Oil Company vessels, which were attacked at the same time, also died. Several British ships were bombed and fired on by shore batteries on the same day. At Tokyo Foreign Minister Hirota immediately tendered the profound apologies of his government, and informed the American Ambassador that the Japanese naval commander at Shanghai had accepted full responsibility. On the day following the incident, Mr. Roosevelt sent a memorandum to Secretary Hull with instructions to inform the Japanese Ambassador that the President "is deeply shocked and concerned by the news of indiscriminate bombing of American and other non-Chinese vessels on the Yangtze, and that he requests that the Emperor be so advised."[30] In the typewritten text of this memorandum, the word "requests" was written in by the President's hand over the original word "suggests." A copy of the memorandum, thus revised, was handed to the press.

Ambassador Grew submitted a formal note at Tokyo on December 14, asserting that previous violations of American rights by Japanese armed forces had occurred despite precautions officially pledged by the Japanese authorities; in the present case, Japan's armed forces had "taken American life" and "destroyed American property both public and private." The American government, therefore, "requests and expects" formal expression of regret, complete indemnification, and an assurance of "definite and specific steps" to ensure American life and property against attack by Japanese armed forces.[31] On the same

[29] For speeches and reports of the conference, see *The Conference of Brussels, November 3-24, 1937*. Washington, Government Printing Office.

[30] State Department, *Press Releases,* December 18, 1937, p. 447.

[31] *Ibid.,* pp. 448-9.

day, in answer to previous representations, Foreign Minister Hirota had transmitted a note through Ambassador Grew which expressed profound regrets and "sincere apologies" for the incident, "entirely due to a mistake," and promised indemnification for losses and appropriate punishment of those responsible.[32] As fuller information became available at Washington, showing conclusively that the attack was not accidental, the American authorities made further representations at Tokyo. A second Japanese note, dated December 24, referred to the previous apology and pledge of indemnification, noted that the Japanese air force commander had been recalled and other officers responsible duly punished, and outlined steps being taken to ensure the safety of American interests and nationals; the incident, however, was still termed a "mistake."[33] On December 25 Secretary Hull accepted this communication as "responsive" to the request made by the American note of December 14, but expressed reliance on the findings of the American naval court of inquiry as to "the origins, causes and circumstances of the incident."[34]

On March 21, 1938 the United States Government presented a claim for $2,214,007.36 in property losses and personal injuries caused by the *Panay* incident. This amount included "no item of punitive damages." One month later, on April 22, after a request for more detailed itemization of the claim had been satisfied, the Japanese government rendered full payment of the amount demanded.[35]

As 1937 ended, the American public was already recovering from the excitement engendered by the *Panay* incident. Considering the type of provocation afforded by this affair, the apparent reaction of popular opinion was unusually mild. Support for the steps taken by the Administration undoubtedly existed, but there was little inclination to press on toward a broader intervention in the Far Eastern conflict. On the contrary, there were continued expressions, both in and out of Congress, of a desire to have American nationals and military-naval contin-

[32] *Ibid.*, pp. 450-1.

[33] State Department, *Press Releases,* December 25, 1937, pp. 497-8.

[34] *Ibid.*, pp. 498-9; also pp. 499-508 for official American reports and naval court inquiry findings on the facts of the incident.

[35] State Department, *Press Releases,* March 26, 1938, p. 410; April 23, p. 504.

gents withdrawn from China. Early in January 1938 a poll by the Gallup Institute showed 70 per cent favoring such withdrawal, whereas only 54 per cent had taken the same stand in September. Senate Resolution No. 210 of January 5, 1938, requesting information as to the numbers of American nationals and armed forces in China, was answered by Secretary Hull on January 8; an earlier letter by Senator Smathers was answered on December 18.[36] In the latter case, Secretary Hull repeated previous assurances that the government was seeking to provide safe means for departure of American nationals from China; the American military and naval forces, however, were still required to assure protection of Americans, and the present did "not seem an opportune moment" for effecting their withdrawal. Partial concessions, nevertheless, were made on January 31, 1938, with announcement that the 1,200 marine reinforcements were returning from Shanghai; while on February 4 it was announced that the Fifteenth Infantry was being withdrawn from Tientsin; at the same time, two of the four companies of the Marine Guard were transferred from Peiping to Tientsin.[37]

Marking Time: From Panay to Munich

During 1937 a rapid succession of diplomatic highlights had centered on the Sino-Japanese conflict, with the United States playing a central role. The tempo of events slowed down considerably in the new year. Having successfully disposed of the *Panay* incident, the Washington authorities seemed content for the moment to adopt an attitude of watchful waiting. This position was rendered the more necessary by the outcome of the Brussels Conference, Anglo-French preoccupation with developments in Europe, and the growing unlikelihood of a speedy peace settlement in the Far East. The narrow defeat of the Ludlow war referendum amendment, voted down in the House by 209 to 188 on January 10, 1938, also predisposed the State Department to move cautiously at this time. As the fighting in China moved inland, moreover, with the larger campaigns occurring around Hsüchow and along the middle Yangtze, there

[36] For texts, see State Department, *Press Releases,* December 25, 1937, pp. 495-6; January 15, 1938, pp. 100-5.

[37] *Ibid.,* February 5, 1938, p. 199-200; February 19, p. 266.

was less immediate danger to a concentrated foreign population such as that located in Shanghai.

Issues of a restricted nature continued to arise over Japanese violations of American business and missionary interests in China. On January 17, 1938, the United States Ambassador at Tokyo presented a note of protest against illegal entry of American property and removal of "goods and employees" by Japanese military forces at Nanking, Hangchow and other places. In these cases, it was charged, Japanese soldiers had disregarded notices posted on the property and "in numerous instances torn down, burned and otherwise mutilated American flags." The note concluded with these sentences:

"In view of the fact that a number of these acts are reported as having occurred subsequent to the receipt of the aforementioned assurances of the Imperial Japanese Government and inasmuch as this disregard of American rights is reported as still continuing, the American Government is constrained to observe that the steps which the Japanese Government have so far taken seem inadequate to ensure that hereafter American nationals, interests and property in China shall not be subjected to attack by Japanese armed forces or unlawful interference by any Japanese authorities or forces whatsoever. My Government must, therefore, request that the Imperial Japanese Government reenforce the instructions which have already been issued in such a way as will serve effectively to prevent the repetition of such outrages."[38]

The Japanese reply to this note, delivered on February 12, pleaded military necessity in extenuation of "mistakes" by requisitioning squads, and noted the "difficulty of ascertaining the facts in circumstances" of a disturbed character. Strict instructions regarding "the importance of respecting the American national emblem" had been sent "to every unit in China;" special officers would be stationed at important points in China "to take charge of matters relating to the rights and interests of third powers;" and the military police in China would be reinforced.[39]

Meanwhile, on January 26, two American citizens at Nanking, including the Third Secretary of the American Embassy, had been "slapped in the face by a Japanese soldier" while in-

[38] State Department, *Press Releases,* January 29, 1938, pp. 177-8.
[39] State Department, *Press Releases,* February 19, 1938, pp. 263-5.

vestigating a case of illegal entry into American property.[40] Representations on this affair, offered by Ambassador Grew on January 29, were promptly answered by the Japanese government. On January 31 the State Department announced acceptance of Japan's expression of "profound regret" for the incident and promise that the responsible parties would be punished.[41]

A more inclusive issue was raised on February 3, when the Japanese Embassy at Peiping warned neutral foreigners to withdraw from a large area of China north of the Yangtze River. The warning, which was transmitted to American and other foreign embassies in Peiping, also desired that neutrals should mark their properties against possible dangers from aerial bombardment before withdrawing. This step amounted, in effect, to a disavowal of Japanese responsibility for damages to foreign property occurring as a result of military operations. Refusal to accept such a contention was made clear in an American note to Japan, the instructions for which were sent to Ambassador Grew on February 18. The substance of this note was outlined by the State Department on February 25 as follows:

"There rests upon American officials and other American nationals in China no obligation whatsoever to take precautionary measures requested on behalf of the contending forces toward safeguarding American lives and interests. Precautionary measures had voluntarily been advised by this government and its officials, and they have been voluntarily undertaken in so far as possible, and such measures will continue voluntarily to be taken. Nevertheless, irrespective of whether American nationals take or do not take such precautionary measures as are suggested, the obligation remains on the Japanese military authorities to exert the utmost precaution to the end that American nationals and property shall not be injured by their military operations. Whether requests of the Japanese military authorities have or have not been complied with, if American nationals or property are injured in consequence of the operations of Japanese armed forces, the United States Government will be compelled to attribute to the government controlling the armed forces responsibility for the damage."[42]

[40] For official report on the facts in this case, see State Department, *Press Releases,* January 29, 1938, pp. 178-81.

[41] State Department, *Press Releases,* February 5, 1938, p. 197.

[42] *New York Times,* February 26, 1938.

Neither the full text of this note nor of the Japanese reply, if and when delivered, was ever made public.

The fact that certain issues growing out of the earlier hostilities at Shanghai and Nanking were still unresolved was made apparent in a protest presented on May 31, 1938 at Tokyo by Ambassador Grew. In this note, the American government expressed its "increasing concern" over the "problem of enabling American citizens to re-enter and repossess" properties from which they had been excluded by the Japanese military. Attention was specifically directed to the University of Shanghai, a Baptist missionary enterprise, which had been occupied by the Japanese military "for a period of nine months," although "hostilities in this locality long ago ceased," and which had suffered looting and damage. Reference was also made to measures preventing American missionaries and businessmen from returning to their places of residence and work in the lower Yangtze valley, although Japanese nationals had been accorded this privilege. In conclusion, the note stated:

"My Government is confident that the Japanese Government cannot but concede that the infringement of and interference with American rights in China by the Japanese authorities involved in the situation to which attention is herein brought are contrary to the repeated assurances of the Japanese Government that the American rights will be respected; that the Japanese Government will take immediate steps, in keeping with such assurances, to cause the return to their rightful owners of the premises of the University of Shanghai and other American property under the occupation of Japanese armed forces; and that the Japanese Government will issue instructions to have removed the obstacles interposed by the Japanese authorities in China against return by American nationals to places such as those mentioned in the areas under Japanese military occupation."[43]

In its reply, which was postponed until July 16, the Japanese government made but partial concession to the American demands. While Japan's armed forces gave up their occupation of Shanghai University, full repossession of the premises by its American owners was denied under plea of military necessity; watchmen would be permitted to reside on the university grounds, and repairs might be effected; as to reparation for

[43] State Department, *Press Releases,* June 4, 1938, pp. 636-7.

damages, "further consideration" would be given this aspect of the question. Conditions in the lower Yangtze valley were still unsettled, making it difficult to permit unrestricted access of foreigners to this region; but, depending upon "actual conditions prevailing in any given place, the policy will be gradually to permit the return of such nationals."[44] Two days later, Secretary Hull indicated that Japan's reply "had not settled the issue to this government's full satisfaction."[45]

During the spring of 1938 the American public was deeply stirred by a series of destructive Japanese air raids on Canton which resulted in heavy loss of civilian life. Increasing attention was drawn to the extent to which American supplies were assisting Japan, and pressure to restrict the sale of bombing planes, in particular, was directed both against Congress and the Administration. A plea for cessation of American economic aid to Japan was made before the General Assembly of the Presbyterian Church on June 1, but the Assembly's report contented itself with a condemnation of "the heedless destruction of the lives and property of innocent non-combatants in many parts of China, most recently evidenced in the bombings of civilians in Canton."[46] Earlier, the annual convention of the New York Conference of the Methodist Episcopal Church had explicitly denounced the policy of the United States in continuing "to buy Japanese goods" and "to sell Japan the materials with which she has been waging aggressive and inexcusable war on China."[47] On June 11 Secretary Hull indicated that the State Department was informally discouraging the sale of American bombing planes to Japan through oral statements made to representatives of American airplane manufacturers.[48] In the same month the Department of Commerce addressed a warning to American exporters containing the following statement: "In view of the increasing severity with which the exchange restrictions in Japan are being enforced, it is believed that a confirmed

[44] *Ibid.*, July 23, 1938, pp. 48-9.

[45] *New York Times,* July 19, 1938.

[46] *New York Herald Tribune,* June 2, 1938.

[47] *Ibid.*, April 24, 1938.

[48] *New York Times,* June 12, 1938. Months later it was revealed that in July 1938 Secretary Hull had sent a letter to all manufacturers of aeronautical equipment stating that the government "strongly opposed" sale of planes and equipment to nations engaged in bombing civilian populations, and would grant licenses for export under such circumstances "with great regret." *Ibid.*, January 10, 1939.

irrevocable letter of credit offers the American exporter the most satisfactory assurance that the Japanese importer has fully complied with the regulations and that payment will be duly forthcoming."[49] A poll of Congressmen conducted at this time by *The Christian Science Monitor* indicated general support for Secretary Hull's effort to discourage shipment of American aircraft to Japan, as well as some sentiment for applying an embargo to a wider range of exports.[50]

Still another American protest was registered at Tokyo on August 26 against "the unwarranted attack on August 24, 1938, near Macao, by Japanese airplanes upon a commercial airplane operated by the China National Aviation Corporation resulting in the total destruction of the commercial airplane, the loss of the lives of a number of non-combatant passengers and the endangering of the life of the American pilot." The note concluded with the sharp statement: "My Government desires to express its emphatic objection to the jeopardizing in this way of the lives of Americans as well as other non-combatant occupants of unarmed civilian planes engaged in clearly recognized and established commercial services over a regularly scheduled air route."[51] The Japanese reply of August 31, while expressing regret for the results of the attack, held it to be "not unwarranted" owing to the fact that the China National Aviation Corporation plane "acted in such a manner as invited suspicions of its being a Chinese military aircraft."[52]

On the eve of the European crisis which culminated in the Munich agreement, a cablegram from the American Chamber of Commerce and the American Community Committee at Shanghai, dated September 2, 1938, revealed that questions which had formed the basis for State Department protests during previous months were still unsettled, and new issues were emerging. The text of the cablegram, which was addressed to the Secretary of State, read as follows:

"Americans in Shanghai, alarmed over the steady progress of the realization of Japanese plans to oust American and other trade from China by means of monopolies, trade and travel restrictions, control of commodities, exchange control, currency

[49] *Christian Science Monitor,* June 22, 1938.
[50] *Ibid.,* June 21, 1938.
[51] State Department, *Press Releases,* August 27, 1938, pp. 146-7.
[52] *New York Times,* September 1, 1938.

manipulation, as already in effect in North China, and crippling the most important lines of American trade there, convinced that the present is the time for America to take a firm stand, insist on:

"1. Restoration of the Shanghai Municipal Council to full authority and control in the International Settlement, including the Hongkew and Yangtzepoo sections;

"2. Restoration of American homes, institutions, business properties and goods to the rightful owners, with full and free access to and use thereof and prompt indemnification for losses;

"3. Discontinuance of Japanese censorship and interference with our mails, telegrams, cables and other means of communication, including radio equipment, now restricted in North China;

"4. Immediate return of equipment and the resumption of dredging operations in the Whangpoo River and Shanghai Harbor in accordance with international agreements;

"5. Restoration of full rights and privileges of trade, travel and residence in the Yangtze Valley, North China and other areas, including the use of railways, shipping, commercial airways and motor highways with access to markets and mission centers on a basis of equal opportunity;

"6. Due respect for and observance of all American treaty rights."

Post-Munich Developments

Significant changes in the Far Eastern military situation occurred during the few weeks which succeeded the Munich agreement. A landing effected by Japanese forces on Bias Bay early in October resulted in the rapid capture of Canton; before the month was out, Hongkong was isolated from Canton and the South China hinterland. The Chinese forces immediately withdrew from the Hankow area, and Hankow also fell to the Japanese army toward the end of October. Shifts in the Tokyo Cabinet, however, as well as statements by Generalissimo Chiang Kai-shek, indicated that the struggle would still be vigorously prosecuted by both sides. The status of foreign interests in China, in the light of these new conditions, was rendered more uncertain than ever; nevertheless, the American government proceeded to initiate at this time a comprehensive diplomatic effort to secure adequate respect for the treaty rights of its citizens.

Under date of October 6, 1938, the American Ambassador delivered to the Japanese government a detailed summary of Japan's continuing violations of the open door principle in China, combined with an implied hint of retaliatory action. After noting inequalities of treatment deriving from exchange control instituted at Tsingtao and in prospect for North China, changes in the Chinese tariffs, monopolistic industrial enterprises set up under Japanese auspices, and various restrictions imposed on individual rights of American nationals in China, the note stated:

"American nationals and their interests have suffered serious losses in the Far East arising from causes directly attributable to the present conflict between Japan and China, and even under the most favorable conditions an early rehabilitation of American enterprise in China and of American trade with China cannot be expected. The American Government, therefore, finds it all the more difficult to reconcile itself to a situation in which American nationals must contend with continuing unwarranted interference with their rights at the hands of the Japanese authorities in China and with Japanese actions and policies which operate to deprive American trade and enterprise of equality of opportunity in China. It is also pertinent to mention that in Japan, too, American trade and other interests are undergoing severe hardships as a result of the industrial, trade, exchange and other controls which the Japanese Government has imposed incident to its military operations in China.

"While American interests in the Far East have been thus treated at the hands of the Japanese authorities, the Government of the United States has not sought either in its own territory or in the territory of third countries to establish or influence the establishment of embargoes, import prohibitions, exchange controls, preferential restrictions, monopolies or special companies designed to eliminate or having the effect of eliminating Japanese trade and enterprise. In its treatment of Japanese nationals and their trade and enterprise, the American Government has been guided not only by the letter and spirit of the Japanese-American Commercial Treaty of 1911 but by those fundamental principles of international law and order which have formed the basis of its policy in regard to all peoples and their interests; and Japanese commerce and enterprise have continued to enjoy in the United States equality of opportunity.

"Your Excellency cannot fail to recognize the existence of a great and growing disparity between the treatment accorded American nationals and their trade and enterprise by Japanese authorities in China and Japan and the treatment accorded Japanese nationals and their trade and enterprise by the Government of the United States in areas within its jurisdiction.

"In the light of the situation herein reviewed, the Government of the United States asks that the Japanese Government implement its assurances already given with regard to the maintenance of the Open Door and to non-interference with American rights by taking prompt and effective measures to cause:

"(1) The discontinuance of discriminatory exchange control and of other measures imposed in areas in China under Japanese control which operate either directly or indirectly to discriminate against American trade and enterprise;

"(2) The discontinuance of any monopoly or of any preference which would deprive American nationals of the right of undertaking any legitimate trade or industry in China, or of any arrangement which might purport to establish in favor of Japanese interests any general superiority of rights with regard to commercial or economic development in any region of China; and

"(3) The discontinuance of interference by Japanese authorities in China with American property and other rights including such forms of interference as censorship of American mail and telegrams, and restrictions upon residence and travel by Americans and upon American trade and shipping.

"The Government of the United States believes that in the interest of relations between the United States and Japan an early reply would be helpful."[53]

The text of this note was released at Washington on October 27; at the time, the Japanese authorities had not yet made response. Japan's reply, finally delivered at the Tokyo Embassy on the evening of November 18, deprecated any intention on the Japanese government's part of discriminating against the

[53] State Department, *Press Releases,* October 29, 1938, pp. 283-6.

rights of American nationals in China, and offered a point-by-point rebuttal of the contentions advanced in the United States note with respect to exchange control measures, revisions of the Chinese tariff, organization of promotion companies, and restrictions on the ordinary privileges of American citizens. It noted that emergency laws affecting American nationals in Japan applied also to the nationals of other states, and reserved "for another occasion" a statement concerning the treatment of Japanese subjects in American territory. The last three paragraphs of the Japanese note contained a most significant pronouncement. They declared:

"Japan at present is devoting her energy to the establishment of a new order based on genuine international justice throughout East Asia, the attainment of which end is not only an indispensable condition of the very existence of Japan, but also constitutes the very foundation of the enduring peace and stability of East Asia.

"It is the firm conviction of the Japanese Government that in the face of the new situation, fast developing in East Asia, any attempt to apply to the conditions of today and tomorrow inapplicable ideas and principles of the past neither would contribute toward the establishment of a real peace in East Asia nor solve the immediate issues.

"However, as long as these points are understood, Japan has not the slightest inclination to oppose the participation of the United States and other powers in the great work of reconstructing East Asia along all lines of industry and trade; and I believe that the new regimes now being formed in China are prepared to welcome such foreign participation."[54]

The American note of October 6 had broadly hinted at the possibility of American economic reprisals, if Japanese infringements of the open door policy in China persisted. The Japanese reply, while denying such infringements, tacitly implied that the principles of the open door policy were no longer applicable to the "new order" which Japan was constructing in East Asia. An *impasse* had apparently been reached.

Confronted with rejection of its previous representations, and a clear Japanese challenge, the United States government resorted—on December 31, 1938—to the dispatch of a second

[54] State Department, *Press Releases,* November 19, 1938, pp. 359-63.

note to Japan, stating its case in even more forceful and comprehensive terms. The American position with regard to the issues raised in the first note was recapitulated in the following terms:

"In the light of facts and experience the Government of the United States is impelled to reaffirm its previously expressed opinion that imposition of restrictions upon the movements and activities of American nationals who are engaged in philanthropic, educational and commercial endeavors in China has placed and will, if continued, increasingly place Japanese interests in a preferred position and is, therefore, unquestionably discriminatory, in its effect, against legitimate American interests. Further, with reference to such matters as exchange control, compulsory currency circulation, tariff revision, and monopolistic promotion in certain areas of China, the plans and practices of the Japanese authorities imply an assumption on the part of those authorities that the Japanese Government or the regimes established and maintained in China by Japanese armed forces are entitled to act in China in a capacity such as flows from rights of sovereignty and, further, in so acting to disregard and even to declare nonexistent or abrogated the established rights and interests of other countries, including the United States."

With respect to Japan's further contentions, the American note, after recalling previous expressions by the United States of its unwillingness to consent to treaty revision by unilateral action, stated:

"In the light of these facts, and with reference especially to the purpose and the character of the treaty provisions from time to time solemnly agreed upon for the very definite purposes indicated, the Government of the United States deprecates the fact that one of the parties to these agreements has chosen to embark—as indicated both by action of its agents and by official statements of its authorities—upon a course directed toward the arbitrary creation by that power by methods of its own selection, regardless of treaty pledges and the established rights of other powers concerned, of a 'new order' in the Far East. Whatever may be the changes which have taken place in the situation in the Far East and whatever may be the situation now, these matters are of no less interest and concern to the American Government than have been the situations which have prevailed there in the past, and such changes as may henceforth take place there, changes which may enter into the producing of a 'new situation' and a 'new order,' are and will be of like concern to this Government. This Government is well aware that the situation has changed. This Government is also well aware that many of the changes have been brought about by action of Japan. This Government does not admit, however, that there is need or warrant for any one power to take upon itself to prescribe what shall be the terms and conditions of a 'new order' in areas not under its sovereignty and to constitute itself the repository of authority and the agent of destiny in regard thereto."

Following this strong statement, the note stressed the previously demonstrated willingness of the United States to modify treaties by orderly "processes of negotiation and agreement," and then concluded:

"The United States has in its international relations rights and obligations which derive from international law and rights and obligations which rest upon treaty provisions. Of those which rest on treaty provisions, its rights and obligations in and with regard to China rest in part upon provisions in treaties between the United States and China, and in part upon provisions in treaties between the United States and several other powers, including both China and Japan. These treaties were concluded in good faith for the purpose of safeguarding and promoting the interests not of one only but of all of their signatories. The people and the Government of the United States cannot assent to the abrogation of any of this country's rights or obligations by the arbitrary action of agents or authorities of any other country.

"The Government of the United States has, however, always been prepared, and is now, to give due and ample consideration to any proposals based on justice and reason which envisage the resolving of problems in a manner duly considerate of the rights and obligations of all parties directly concerned by processes of free negotiation and new commitment by and among all of the parties so concerned. There has been and there continues to be opportunity for the Japanese Government to put forward such proposals. This Government has been and it continues to be willing to discuss such proposals, if and when put forward, with representatives of the other powers, including Japan and China, whose rights and interests are involved, at whatever time and in whatever place may be commonly agreed upon.

"Meanwhile, this Government reserves all rights of the United States as they exist and does not give assent to any impairment of any of those rights."[55]

Although this note contained no suggestion of possible retaliatory measures, it was not left altogether without the support of specific action.[56] Two weeks earlier, on December 15, the United States Export-Import Bank had placed a credit of $25 million at China's disposal; in addition, the Treasury had extended the Chinese-American monetary agreement of July 9, 1937 by which China was enabled to dispose of its silver and obtain dollar exchange against its gold reserves thus accumulated in New York. And less than a week later, on January 4, 1939, in the President's annual message to Congress, the following statements were made:

"We have learned that God-fearing democracies of the world which observe the sanctity of treaties and good faith in their dealings with other nations cannot be safely indifferent to international lawlessness anywhere. They cannot forever let pass, without effective protest, acts of aggression against sister nations—acts which automatically undermine all of us.

"Obviously they must proceed along practical, peaceful lines. But the mere fact that we rightly decline to intervene with arms to prevent acts of aggression does not mean that we must act as if there were no aggression at all. Words may be futile, but war is not the only means of commanding a decent respect for the opinions of mankind. There are many methods short of war, but stronger and more effective than mere words, of bringing home to aggressor governments the aggregate sentiments of our own people.

"At the very least, we can and should avoid any action, or any lack of action, which will encourage, assist or build up an aggressor. We have learned that when we deliberately try to legislate neutrality, our neutrality laws may operate unevenly and unfairly—may actually give aid to an aggressor and deny it to

[55] State Department, *Press Releases,* December 31, 1938, pp. 490-3.

[56] The note was reinforced by protests, similar in tenor, delivered at Tokyo by Great Britain and France in the middle of January.

the victim. The instinct of self-preservation should warn us that we ought not to let that happen any more."[57]

In tone and substance, this statement recalled the emphasis of the President's Chicago speech of October 5, 1937. Both addresses constituted a warning to aggressors and a defense of the need for concerted international action to safeguard peace. The message to Congress, however, looked much more directly toward revision of the Neutrality Act, and in this respect accorded with a change in the temper of public sentiment.

The Munich agreement of the previous autumn had led to the first pronounced shift in American opinion on foreign policy since 1935. During the first six months of 1939, events both in Europe and the Far East again brought home to the American people the threat of general war. In contrast to earlier periods, the normal reaction toward a strengthening of isolationist sentiment did not occur. Germany's partition of Czechoslovakia in March 1939, and the strokes of the axis powers in Memel, Rumania and Albania, reinforced the trend against mandatory neutrality legislation. A series of polls by the Gallup Institute showed 34 per cent voting for the sale of arms to England and France before Munich, 55 per cent in March 1939, and 66 per cent in April 1939. The American Union for Concerted Peace Efforts, formed in the spring of 1939, directed the activity of a considerable number of peace organizations toward winning the support of the United States for measures to check the spread of aggression. While the reaction in Congress was not so pronounced, it was clear that there, too, the neutrality advocates were losing ground.

The spread of aggression in Europe had been matched in the Far East by Japan's occupation of Hainan Island in February and of the Spratly Islands in March—political moves which served to emphasize the growing Japanese pressure against Western economic interests in China. An increasing body of American opinion tended to question the advisability of permitting vast amounts of war materials to be sold to Japan, when the latter's activities were jeopardizing American interests and meeting with the official opposition of Washington. Secretary Hull's attempts to halt the sale of American aircraft to Japan, as well as the Export-Import Bank's loan to China, met with

[57] *New York Times,* January 5, 1939.

little opposition, although both steps moved beyond the range of a strictly neutral attitude. Organization of the American Committee for Non-Participation in Japanese Aggression, headed by Mr. Henry L. Stimson, stimulated to activity and focused upon Congress the existing but inchoate sentiment which favored positive measures to curb Japan. The Conference on the Cause and Cure of War, meeting at Washington in January 1939, went on record for the first time in favor of an embargo on war materials to Japan. In May 1939 the General Assembly of the Presbyterian Church, reversing its neutral attitude of the previous year, adopted a resolution condemning America's continued "partnership in aggression" and urging immediate legislation by Congress to prevent the sale of munitions and war materials to Japan.[58]

Reconsideration of the neutrality statute by Congress progressed slowly during the early part of the session, with the Administration adopting a "hands-off" attitude. Public hearings on revision of the act were not concluded until May; meanwhile, on May 1, 1939, the "cash-and-carry" provisions had expired. Toward the end of the month Secretary Hull, in conference with members of the House, moved definitely to secure elimination of the mandatory arms embargo. On June 13 a bill framed along lines supported by the State Department was reported out by the House Foreign Affairs Committee. This bill extended the "cash-and-carry" principle to all commodities, thus eliminating the arms embargo, and broadened the President's discretionary powers. At the end of June a bi-partisan coalition in the House forced through an amendment restoring the arms embargo—a move which defeated the Administration's prime objective. On June 30 the House passed the bill in this modified form by a vote of 200 to 188.

There still remained the possibility of action by the Senate, and during the early weeks of July the battleground of neutrality revision shifted to the Senate Foreign Relations Committee. The actual decision, as it turned out, was rendered on July 11 when the Committee, by a vote of 12 to 11, refused to report to the Senate a measure calling for repeal of the mandatory arms embargo in favor of a general "cash-and-carry" program.[59] On

[58] *New York Times*, June 1, 1939.

[59] Senators voting against: Democrats—Bennett Champ Clark (Missouri), Walter F. George (Georgia), Guy M. Gillette (Iowa), Frederick Van Nuys (Indiana),

July 14, in an effort to break the deadlock, President Roosevelt transmitted to Congress a carefully prepared brief for neutrality revision by Secretary Hull.[60] Several days later, after conferences with Republican and Democratic leaders, the President reluctantly abandoned hope of forcing further action in the Senate. He declared his belief, however, that Congressional failure to revise the neutrality statute increased the danger of war in Europe, and indicated that he would call a special session of Congress in the event of a major European crisis.

The session thus ended with a truncated Neutrality Act, minus the previous "cash-and-carry" provisions covering shipments of commodities other than arms, on the statute books. Under these conditions, in case of a European conflict, shipments of American munitions of war to belligerent powers would be embargoed, while shipments of other American commodities would continue on a normal basis unrestricted by "cash-and-carry" provisions.

By the spring of 1939 Japan's trade relations with the United States had become an important issue, and were being subjected to close scrutiny by an increasing proportion of the American public. The sale of Japanese goods to the United States had markedly declined in 1938. Whereas the value of American imports from Japan had totaled $204 million in 1937, it had dropped to $127 million in 1938. The exact degree to which boycott sentiment had contributed to this decline of $77 million is conjectural; that the boycott had played a significant role, however, seems clear. American exports to Japan showed no comparable decline, being valued at $289 million in 1937 and $240 million in 1938. A careful analysis of the commodities in this export trade which may be termed essential for war purposes is given in the accompanying table.

Robert R. Reynolds (North Carolina); Republicans—William H. Borah (Idaho), Hiram Johnson (California), Arthur Capper (Kansas), Arthur H. Vandenberg (Michigan), Wallace H. White (Maine); Progressive—Robert M. La Follette (Wisconsin); Farmer-Laborite—Henrik Shipstead (Minnesota).

Senators voting for: Democrats—Key Pittman (Nevada), Pat Harrison (Mississippi), Robert F. Wagner (New York), Tom Connally (Texas), Elbert D. Thomas (Utah), James E. Murray (Montana), Lewis B. Schwellenbach (Washington), Claude Pepper (Florida), Theodore F. Green (Rhode Island), Alben W. Barkley (Kentucky), Joseph F. Guffey (Pennsylvania).

[60] Text in State Department. *Bulletin,* July 15, 1939, pp. 43-7.

PERCENTAGE SHARE OF INDIVIDUAL ITEMS IN TOTAL VALUE OF U. S. EXPORTS TO JAPAN ESSENTIAL FOR WAR PURPOSES*

Commodity	*1938* Value (\$1,000)	*1938* Per cent of Total	*1937* Value (\$1,000)	*1937* Per cent of Total
Total	171,574	100.00	173,010	100.00
Petroleum and products†	53,136	30.97	44,900	25.95
Metal-working machinery†	24,455	14.25	12,224	7.06
Copper	22,164	12.92	19,212	11.10
Iron and steel scrap	22,061	12.86	39,386	22.76
Aircraft and parts‡	17,454	10.17	2,484	1.44
Automobiles, parts and accessories†	12,050	7.02	15,206	8.79
Iron and steel semi-manufactures§	6,366	3.71	23,005	13.30
Pig iron	4,886	2.85	9,672	5.59
Hides and skins	2,652	1.54	2,691	1.56
Ferro-alloys	2,332	1.36	1,366	0.79
Lead	2,100	1.22	754	0.44
Internal combustion engines†	543	0.32	539	0.31
Aluminum	476	0.28	280	0.16
Non-ferrous metals§	320	0.19	95	0.05
Scrap rubber	250	0.14	171	0.10
Nickel	157	0.09	219	0.13
Arms and ammunition	100	0.06	49	0.03
Leather	45	0.03	703	0.41
Zinc	27	0.02	54	0.03

* Source: Hu Tun-Yuan, Statistical Excerpts from *Japan's Problem of Procurement of Strategic War Materials,* The Chinese Council for Economic Research, Washington, D. C.

† Including shipments to Kwantung, Manchuria.

‡ 1938 figure includes shipments to Shanghai.

§ Not elsewhere specified.

The above table includes approximately \$20 million in materials essential for war purposes sold to Manchukuo in 1937-8. With these items eliminated, a classified summary of direct United States exports to Japan during 1937-8 would show the following proportions for the three main heads.

Classification	*1937*	*1938*	*1937–1938*
Total exports	\$288,558,000	\$239,575,000	\$528,133,000
War materials	167,962,000	158,527,000	326,489,000
Raw cotton	61,724,000	52,644,000	114,368,000
Other exports	58,872,000	28,404,000	87,276,000

In the hearings on the Neutrality Act a fairly wide public demand had, for the first time, forced consideration of the bearing of neutrality legislation on the Far Eastern situation. Several bills placing limitations on Japan's trade with the United States were offered by members of both Houses. In the case of a resolution sponsored by Senator Pittman which empowered the

President to impose an embargo on war supplies to Japan, the Senate Foreign Relations Committee requested Secretary Hull to indicate whether such action "would violate any treaty." Replying to this request on July 21, Mr. Hull stated:

"In the light of the legislative situation relating to this and kindred proposals in regard to our foreign relations, it is reasonably apparent that there is a disposition in Congress to defer until the next session full and final consideration of proposed legislation on this general subject. Furthermore, as an early adjournment of Congress appears to be tacitly agreed upon, it seems clear that there may not be sufficient time in which to consider and enact legislation such as is proposed.

"In these circumstances, I venture respectfully to inquire whether comment by the Department of State on the various proposals pertaining to this phase of our foreign relations could not be offered to a better advantage when Congress at its next session is ready to give full consideration to these and related proposals."[61]

This statement effectively laid to rest any immediate possibility of embargo action against Japan, even though it evaded an answer to the main query. On the same date, however, in answer to a request for his views on a resolution by Senator Vandenberg proposing denunciation of the Japanese-American commercial treaty of 1911 and reassembly of the Brussels Conference of 1937, Secretary Hull wrote:

"Notwithstanding the authority which is vested in the Executive in regard to the matters mentioned in the resolution, I am glad to say that the Executive is always pleased to have advice from the Senate and to give such advice full and careful consideration consonant with the great weight to which the opinions of the Senate are entitled. Such consideration will, therefore, be given to the opinion of the Senate as set forth in the resolution under reference, in the event of its passage."[62]

While the latter response appeared non-committal, it actually preceded State Department action on the trade treaty by only five days. This step was taken at a critical stage in a new crisis which Japan's aggressive encroachments on Western interests had brought about in the Far East during the spring and summer of 1939.

[61] State Department, *Bulletin,* July 22, 1939, p. 61.
[62] *Ibid.*

In May a storm, long brewing over the foreign concessions and settlements in China, had broken out in full force. For several months the local Japanese authorities at Shanghai and Tientsin had been exerting strenuous efforts to establish greater control over the foreign-administered areas in those cities. Early in March a tense situation at Shanghai had been smoothed over, but the compromise then reached was obviously temporary. On May 3 the Vice-Minister for Foreign Affairs at Tokyo submitted an *aide-mémoire* to the British and American Ambassadors; at the time, the text of this communication was not published, but the American reply later revealed that it raised basic issues with regard to administrative control of the International Settlement at Shanghai.

Before this reply was delivered, direct Japanese pressure on the foreign settlements and concessions was intensified. Local Japanese authorities, both civil and military, renewed the agitation previously conducted at Shanghai and Tientsin. On May 12 a force of Japanese marines was landed at Kulangsu, island center of the International Settlement at Amoy, ostensibly to deal with the shooting of a local Chinese puppet official. Immediately after the occupation, however, extensive demands for revision of the Kulangsu administration were presented to the foreign authorities of the Settlement. These events, it was immediately recognized, provided a test case for the larger issues at stake in Shanghai and Tientsin. Several Western naval vessels were concentrated at the island, and on May 17-18 American, British and French patrols, each equal to the Japanese force, were landed at Kulangsu. On May 19 both foreign areas at Shanghai mustered an impressive display of all available military, naval and police forces, which undertook a search for terrorists and concealed arms. As at Kulangsu, this display of force was clearly designed as a warning to Japan; these vigorous measures succeeded in postponing further Japanese moves for nearly a month.

The American reply to the Japanese *aide-mémoire* had meanwhile reached Tokyo on May 17. While the note was conciliatory in tone, it nevertheless amounted to a firm rejection of the Japanese demands. The American government declared itself ready to participate in "friendly and orderly negotiations properly instituted and conducted" for any needed revision of the Settlement's land regulations. Present abnormal conditions, however, offered no basis for "an orderly settlement of the complicated problems involved which would be reasonably fair to all concerned." The United States rejected Tokyo's demand for revision of the voting system, on the ground that the Japanese community already enjoyed a proportionately greater vote than that to which it was entitled by virtue of the municipal rates and land taxes it paid. Adjustments of the Settlement's administrative practice had been made in the past, and the American government felt that similar attempts to meet "any reasonable requests" would continue. The efforts of the Settlement officials to perform their normal functions, however, had been "seriously handicapped" by "lawless activities in areas contiguous to the International Settlement and by refusal on the part of the Japanese military forces to return the Settlement area lying north of Soochow Creek to the effective control of the authorities of the International Settlement." Smooth functioning of the Settlement's administrative machinery would be promoted by a "frank recognition" on Japan's part of the excellent work of the Settlement authorities and "by the prompt restoration to those authorities of complete control over the Settlement area extending north of Soochow Creek."[63]

Two aspects of this preliminary episode in the struggle over the foreign-controlled areas deserve notice. For purposes of direct defense interests threatened by Japanese encroachment, the United States had showed itself prepared to make at least a display of armed force. In contrast to the situation prevailing in 1937, this action caused no outcry in the United States; on the contrary, it met with general public approval. In the second place, the American action was supported by the European powers directly concerned. French and British, as well as American, forces were landed at Kulangsu; French, British and American forces co-operated in the armed display at Shanghai; and the American rejection of the demands in the Japanese *aide-mémoire* was closely followed by a similar British rejection, delivered at Tokyo on May 19. Like parallels had occurred during preceding months, notably in the case of the British and French notes of January 1939 and of the British loan of £5 million to China in March, both of which followed a course of action previously taken by the United States. These steps indicated that

[63] State Department, *Press Releases,* May 20, 1939, pp. 421-3.

the Western powers were developing an increasing measure of co-operation on Far Eastern questions.

The effectiveness with which such co-operation could be applied in the Far East was subjected to a further test in June, when the brunt of the Japanese attack on the foreign concessions was transferred to Tientsin. Making use of the detention of four alleged Chinese terrorists in the British Concession, the local Japanese authorities established a blockade of the foreign-controlled areas, both British and French, on June 14. In this case, Japan made a strong effort to single out Britain for special attack, with the obvious intention of splitting the united Anglo-American-French front which had formed in defense of the Shanghai and Kulangsu Settlements. Passing far beyond the immediate issue, demands by Japanese spokesmen called upon Great Britain to co-operate with Japan in setting up the "new order" in East Asia. While American nationals held a sizable business stake at Tientsin, the United States possessed no jurisdictional rights in the concessions. At the same time, it was clear that American and French interests in China would be undermined to the extent that Japan's aims in the attack on Britain were realized. On June 19, in a statement issued at his press conference, Secretary Hull pointedly alluded to this basic consideration:

"This Government is not concerned in the original incident at Tientsin relating to the requested delivery of the four accused Chinese. It is concerned, however, with the nature and significance of subsequent developments, in their broader aspects, coupled with other past and present acts and utterances in other parts of China. This Government, therefore, is observing with special interest all related developments in China as they occur from day to day. I have nothing further to add today."[64]

Secretary Hull's statement was supported by two protests delivered on the same day at Tokyo. In the first case, the American *Chargé d'Affaires* protested the Japanese naval blockade established June 15 against the Kulangsu Settlement at Amoy, where the United States possesses a direct jurisdictional interest. In the second case, the *Chargé d'Affaires* requested permission to publish an exchange of notes, and made further oral representations, concerning Japanese bombings of American properties in

[64] State Department, *Press Releases,* June 24, 1939, p. 541.

China. While this move was not directly concerned with the issues at Amoy or Tientsin, it served to emphasize continuing American opposition to Japan's activities in China. On June 21, moreover, Secretary Hull announced that the American Consul-General in Tientsin, utilizing a statement drawn up by the local American Chamber of Commerce, had formally objected to the adverse effects of the blockade on the interests and general welfare of the American nationals in the city. Finally, on June 22, Admiral Yarnell, Commander-in-Chief of the American Asiatic fleet, bluntly rejected a Japanese demand that American nationals and naval vessels be withdrawn from Swatow, which Japanese military forces had just occupied. Similar action was taken by the British naval commander, and additional British and American naval vessels were dispatched to Swatow.

At Tientsin, nevertheless, the blockade instituted by the Japanese army authorities was intensified. The stripping and searching of British nationals at the Tientsin barricades aroused public opinion in Britain and called forth vigorous official statements, but, mindful of the German threat in Europe, the British authorities showed no inclination to adopt measures of economic reprisal against Japan. Instead, efforts were directed toward securing some form of local settlement. The initial British effort to obtain a neutral review of the evidence concerning the four accused Chinese, through a committee under the chairmanship of the American Consul-General at Tientsin, met with a brusque rebuff from Japan. By mid-July the pressure on Great Britain at Tientsin had become virtually intolerable, and unofficial Japanese demands of broad scope were being voiced. In the face of all provocations, British diplomacy still bent its energies toward localizing the dispute. Preliminary talks between Foreign Minister Hachiro Arita and the British Ambassador, Sir Robert Leslie Craigie, began in Tokyo on July 15 and continued at intervals for more than a week. On July 24 the text of a basic accord under which negotiations would be conducted for a formal settlement of the Tientsin dispute was announced in London. This significant Craigie-Arita formula ran as follows:

"His Majesty's Government in the United Kingdom fully recognize the actual situation in China where hostilities on a large scale are in progress, and note that, as long as that state of affairs continues to exist, the Japanese forces in China have special requirements for the purpose of safeguarding their own security and maintaining public order in regions under their control, and that they have to suppress or remove any such causes or acts as will obstruct them or benefit their enemy.

"His Majesty's Government have no intention of countenancing any acts or measures prejudicial to the attainment of the above-mentioned objects by the Japanese forces, and they will take this opportunity to confirm their policy in this respect by making it plain to British authorities and British nationals in China that they should refrain from such acts and measures."[65]

On the face of it, this document made extensive concessions to Japan, notably in recognizing the Japanese army's "special requirements" in areas of China occupied during the course of an undeclared war. Yet the phraseology of the accord was sufficiently vague to relegate its final results to whatever agreements might be reached in negotiations conducted under the formula itself. At the outset it was clear that Japan expected much from the accord. Its publication followed immediately upon the setback to neutrality revision at Washington and subsequent elimination of the possibility of a Congressional embargo on shipments of American war supplies to Japan at that moment. On July 26, however, only two days after announcement of the Craigie-Arita formula, Secretary Hull served notice of denunciation of the Japanese-American commercial treaty.[66] Official Japanese reactions at once indicated the gravity attached to the State Department's move by Tokyo, which had consistently discounted the possibility of substantial efforts to curb sales of United States war materials to Japan.

As six months were required to give effect to the denunciation of the trade treaty, no immediate action to stop the flow of American war materials to Japan was envisaged at Washington. Specific moves in this direction were unlikely to occur until the next regular session of Congress.[67] On the other hand, Secretary Hull's action constituted a serious warning to Japan, while indirectly it tended to strengthen Britain's hands in the important negotiations being instituted under the Craigie-Arita accord.

This latter effect did not become immediately apparent at

[65] *The Times* (London), July 25, 1939.

[66] For text, see State Department, *Bulletin,* July 29, 1939, p. 81.

[67] The results of a Gallup poll, announced August 30, showed over 80 per cent supporting denunciation of the treaty and favoring embargo measures when the treaty expired.

Tokyo. The first stages of the Anglo-Japanese negotiations, confined mainly to policing issues in the British Concession at Tientsin, passed off satisfactorily. On August 11, the British government decided that the four accused Chinese should be handed over for trial to the local Chinese courts, which are dominated by Japan, at Tientsin.[68] Certain other agreements were also reached affecting co-operation between the Japanese army and the authorities of the British Concession at Tientsin for suppression of terrorism and maintenance of order, subject to final settlement on points of detail. But when the Japanese delegates proceeded to demand surrender of Chinese silver deposited at Tientsin, as well as suppression of the circulation of the Chinese national currency in the Concession, the conference struck a snag. After some delay, the British conferees decided to take further time for consultation with the governments of France and the United States. On August 18, acting on instructions from London following these consultations at Washington and Paris, Ambassador Craigie informed the Japanese negotiators that, in any further discussions respecting the silver and currency questions, arrangements would have to be made to take into account the views of other interested powers. This position was set forth in detail by a Foreign Office statement issued on August 20 at London.[69]

The renewed evidence of Anglo-American-French co-operation on Far Eastern issues, revealed in these developments, led to some signs of hesitancy at Tokyo. For the moment, at least, it appeared that the Anglo-Japanese negotiations had reached an *impasse*, and that, too, before the British had been induced to surrender any vital positions. In China, however, the Japanese army immediately undertook new measures of reprisal against Britain. Flood waters had temporarily disrupted the blockade of the Tientsin concessions, but ominous moves were noted both at Shanghai, where 6,000 Japanese troops were landed following

[68] *The Bulletin of International News* (Royal Institute of International Affairs, London), August 26, 1939, p. 21. At London official explanations indicated that the Law Officers of the Crown, "after studying evidence against the men supplied confidentially by the Japanese authorities on July 30, had come to the conclusion that it constituted a *prima facie* case against two of the men on a charge of murder, and against the other two on a charge of membership of an illegal organisation." This decision has been challenged by the action of certain private British nationals in applying for a writ of *habeas corpus*.

[69] For these details of the negotiations, see *ibid.*, pp. 18-22.

an affray in which a British sergeant acting in self-defense killed two men of the local Japanese-dominated police force, and at Hongkong, where Japanese troops occupied the area along the mainland borders of the Kowloon leased territory. Following announcement of the Soviet-German non-agression pact, however, these activities at Shanghai and Hongkong were suddenly called off, while the Anglo-Japanese negotiations at Tokyo were left in a state of suspended animation.

CHAPTER VIII

THE AMERICAN INTEREST IN THE FAR EASTERN CRISIS

Events occurring in East Asia since 1931 have forced the United States government to restate and reassert the basic principles of American Far Eastern policy. The new set of American state papers appearing during recent years has constituted, in effect, a reaffirmation of traditional objections which the United States has pursued in the Far East since the nineteenth century.

A superficial reading of contemporary United States notes addressed to Japan, especially during the past year, might lead to the belief that they are merely concerned with the troubles of a few American nationals in a remote quarter of the globe. In fact, the American stake in the Sino-Japanese conflict is of far greater importance than such a judgment would suggest. By dint of repetition, the terms "equality of opportunity," the "open door," and the "territorial integrity" of China have sometimes come to seem little more than shibboleths. But these phrases sum up an official attitude toward Far Eastern questions from which the American government has not deviated since 1899, and the roots of which can be traced back to a much earlier period. When the realities which lie behind these phrases have been challenged, the American government has not sought to enforce them by reckless and irresponsible resort to armed force. Yet it has never surrendered them.

After 1915 a period of nearly seven years ensued before the Washington treaties were signed in February 1922. The Nine-Power Treaty fully satisfied the requirements of American policy, which essentially sought two objectives: opportunity for all nations to participate on equal terms in the commercial and industrial development of China, and opportunity for China to develop and maintain a stable and independent government. In one form or another, for nearly eight years, Japan has been violating its commitments under this treaty; more recently, the Japanese authorities have implicitly disowned it. The American government has refrained from any attempt to enforce the Nine-Power Treaty by other than pacific methods. Even "measures short of war" have been eschewed. It has called attention to violations of the rights of American nationals. It has asserted the continuing validity of the principles underlying the Nine-Power Treaty. It shows no sign of giving up these principles.

The economic issues at stake for the United States in the Sino-Japanese conflict, when narrowly restricted to a summation of American trade and investment relations with China, appear relatively unimportant. In 1928-9, American trade with China aggregated $250 million annually; in 1937 it amounted to but $150 million, exclusive of $30 million with Hongkong. American investments in China came to approximately $250 million in 1937, including some $50 million in missionary and philanthropic institutions. Although these sums represent but a fractional part of total American trade and investment, they are hardly negligible under present world economic conditions. Several additional factors, moreover, have to be considered before the economic stake of the United States in the current Far Eastern situation is dismissed by reference to the above figures.

In 1937 approximately 12,000 American nationals were resident in China. The majority of these were connected with some 400 American business concerns in that country, while several thousand Americans were engaged in missionary enterprises built up by more than a century of effort. In recent years, the United States has held the leading position in China's import and export trade, and it is reasonable to believe that this position would have been maintained. In 1937, with good prospects of continued political stability, China was beginning to import considerable amounts of capital goods for a large-scale plan of modernization and industrial development. The United States, with much of its productive capacity lying idle, was in a position to benefit considerably from such a program of modernization in China.

The Sino-Japanese conflict has not only cut short this prospect and worked enormous damage to property, both Chinese and foreign. It has substituted the possibility of an entirely different course of development—one leading to the establishment of a Japan-China-Manchukuo economic bloc, or a regional economy administered under Japanese auspices. Judging by past experience, the economic outlook for the United States under such a regime would not be favorable. American exports to Manchuria fell from $14,600,000 in 1929 to an average of $7,710,000 in 1932-6—a period when Manchukuo was carrying on a large railway construction program. The drop was far greater than in American trade with China proper during the same years, and considerably more than the relative decline in total American trade. In this period, moreover, American business concerns in Manchuria were almost entirely eliminated by state monopolies established with the aid of Japanese capital, thus reducing the degree of independent access to this market formerly possessed. The same technique is now being applied in China proper, with the same results. American business and trade cannot long hope to survive the application of such measures as "exchange control, compulsory currency circulation, tariff revision, and monopolistic promotion" companies, as well as "restrictions upon the movements and activities of American nationals," as cited in the United States note of December 31, 1938.

It is sometimes asserted that China, if subjected to complete Japanese control, would undergo an industrial evolution that would redound to the advantage of the United States. All evidence, past and present, tends to refute this assertion. Only an independent China can be expected to undertake and carry to completion a fully rounded program of economic development. Japan's essential objective, as official declarations of its statesmen have indicated, is to create a regional economy that would reduce Japan's dependence on the outside world. In such a system, China's role—and that of its people—is obvious. It would be a market for Japanese goods and a source of supply to Japan for raw materials, mineral and agricultural; certain export industries, such as textiles, would also be carried forward with the cheap and abundant Chinese labor. In several major respects, the United States would probably suffer severely from such a program. Not only would it lose its present export-import trade with China, and meet even more strenuous competition in the textile field. The expansion of cotton growing in China, plans for which have been worked out by Japanese technical experts, would eliminate the major American export commodity to Japan—raw cotton. To the extent that Japan succeeds in establishing the Japan-China-Manchukuo economic bloc, in other words, the United States would find its trade both with China and Japan correspondingly reduced. The "regionalizing" of world economy would be carried one step further, with results bound to be prejudicial to efforts directed at freeing the flow of international trade and reversing the trend toward economic nationalism.

In the more purely political phase of the Sino-Japanese conflict, also, the United States has an interest at stake that is far broader than its expression in terms of treaty rights. Until recent years, the issue of China's independence and territorial and administrative integrity was usually regarded as a subordinate corollary to the open door policy. The Nine-Power Treaty expressly bound its signatories to respect both principles. Present conditions, by demonstrating how closely equality of commercial opportunity is dependent on China's independence, have placed the latter in the primary position. But this second principle has a far more significant application under modern conditions. It is the key to an enduring Far Eastern peace. Unless the independence of China is firmly established, there can be no real or lasting measure of stability in the Far East. The forces of Chinese nationalism have spread too wide and gone too deep to permit of a *pax Japonica* in East Asia. So long as Japan persists in efforts directed toward that end, the Far East will continue to be a zone of strife and unsettlement.

In the present period of general insecurity, moreover, consideration of the political issue, as it affects the United States, cannot be limited solely to Sino-Japanese relationships and to the Far East. Crisis in the Far East has its setting in a world crisis. In his address before the National Press Club on March 17, 1938, Secretary Hull declared:

". . . the interest and concern of the United States—whether in the Far East, in any other part of the Pacific area, in Europe, or anywhere else in the world—are not measured alone by the number of American citizens residing in a particular country, or by the volume of investment and trade, or by exceptional conditions peculiar to the particular area. There is a much broader and more fundamental interest—which is, that orderly processes in international relationships based on the principles to which I have referred be maintained. . . . The catastrophic developments of recent years, the startling events of the past weeks, offer a tragic demonstration of how quickly the contagious scourge of treaty breaking and armed violence spreads from one region to another. Those who contend that we can and should abandon and surrender principles in one-half of the world clearly show that they have little or no conception of the extent to which situations and developments in any part of the world of today inevitably affect situations and conditions in other parts of the world."[1]

The argument is sometimes advanced that the security of the United States is not directly or immediately threatened by the Sino-Japanese conflict. But this is to conceive of events in the Far East in artificial isolation from events in the rest of the world. For three years the tide of aggression rose steadily higher in Europe; in September 1939, a large-scale conflict was precipitated. It could hardly be maintained that the security of the United States would remain unaffected by a complete success of aggression, both in Europe and Asia. The political interest of the United States in the Far Eastern conflict is, in fact, part and parcel of its general interest in the maintenance of world stability and peace.

[1] State Department, Publication No. 1146, pp. 12-13.

CHAPTER IX

EXPIRATION OF THE TRADE TREATY: THE NEW STATUS

Six months of war in Europe have changed the international setting of the Far Eastern conflict in a number of major respects. In July 1939, when Secretary Hull denounced the Japanese-American commercial treaty, Japan was carrying the attack to third powers in the Far East all along the line. The issues raised by the Tientsin blockade, and by earlier Japanese moves at Shanghai and Amoy, affected Britain, France and the United States in almost equal degree.[1] During the summer of 1939 Japan was also engaged in severe military conflict with the U.S.S.R. on the Outer Mongolian frontier. For diplomatic support of this seemingly over-extended position, Japan was relying on its association with Germany and Italy in the anti-Comintern pact. The army extremists were vigorously campaigning to transform the loose Japanese entente with the Rome-Berlin axis into an outright military alliance.

Japan's international position changed almost overnight as a result of the Soviet-German non-aggression treaty, Germany's invasion of Poland, and the ensuing European war. The U.S.S.R., freed from the threat of combined German-Japanese action, was enabled to deploy far greater strength against Japan in the Far East. The United States, as the result of Japan's increased measure of dependence on the American market, could bring even stronger economic pressure to bear—particularly in view of denunciation of the trade treaty. Britain and France were further immobilized in the Far East, but Japan could not exploit this secondary factor effectively in the face of the cardinal access of strength to the positions of the Soviet Union and the United States. (This judgment, however, only holds true if the United States is prepared to use its power against Japan. If not, Britain and France may prove willing and able to conclude an agreement with Japan directed against the

[1] Cf. pp. 87-91

Soviet Union. China would thereby be sacrificed, and the historic objectives of American Far Eastern policy jeopardized.) Tokyo promptly recognized the diplomatic necessities of the changed situation, which amounted to relative international isolation for Japan's adventure in conquest. Under a new Cabinet, headed by General Abe, Japan moderated its attitude toward Britain, signed a truce to border hostilities with the Soviet Union, and sought to conciliate the United States.

During the past six months, Japanese diplomacy has consistently adhered to the program thus laid down in September, 1939. Establishment of the "new order in East Asia" still stands as Japan's goal, but policy has been tempered to meet the increasing difficulties of its position.

Growing differences between the major Far Eastern powers—France and Britain, the Soviet Union, and the United States—have facilitated Tokyo's diplomacy. Instead of putting forth a concerted effort to settle the Sino-Japanese conflict, which could now be made with maximum possibility of success, Japan's various opponents have drifted into a subtle game of diplomatic point counter point. In the autumn of 1939 Britain and France withdrew the bulk of their troops from North China, while most of the British gunboats were taken off the Yangtze River. These moves obviously constituted pronounced gestures of good will toward Japan. Since then the growing hostility of the Anglo-French bloc to the U.S.S.R. has strengthened forces tending toward emergence of an Anglo-French-Japanese entente. If the war in Europe is intensified, Anglo-French desire for a general understanding with Japan will undoubtedly increase. Japan may hope to repeat the history of the last war, when its secret treaties with the Allied powers helped to consolidate territorial gains won by force of arms.

Reacting to the possibility of a Far Eastern Munich, the Soviet Union has coupled its military aid to China with an effort to restore its relations with Japan to normal. By the end of 1939 the U.S.S.R. was supplying the bulk of China's imports of war supplies. At the same time, it was responding to Japan's evident willingness to settle outstanding Soviet-Japanese issues, following the latter's severe military setback on the Outer Mongolian frontier. A series of arrangements was being concluded with regard to fisheries, territorial boundaries, and trade relations. The possibility of a non-aggression pact lay in the background.

In this new international setting of Far Eastern issues, the United States had not departed essentially from the lines of previous American policy. The customary deliberate and cautious tactics were still being pursued, despite one or two dramatic accompaniments.

Ambassador Grew's outspoken address,[2] delivered before the America-Japan Society in Tokyo on October 19, 1939, was a striking maneuver. It undoubtedly achieved its main objective of reaching a large section of the Japanese public with a statement of the American position. In this important respect, the Ambassador's speech was far more effective than the notes of October 6 or December 31, 1938 had been. Many Japanese heard for the first time that "American public opinion with regard to recent and current developments in the Far East is today very nearly unanimous," and that it "strongly resents some of the things which Japan's armed forces are doing in China today, including actions against American rights and legitimate interests in China." Others may have learned that the "American government and people understand what is meant by 'the new order in East Asia'," that "the new order has appeared to include, among other things, depriving Americans of their long-established rights in China," and that "to this the American people are opposed." Yet these statements added nothing to the earlier notes, and the Ambassador's failure to refer specifically to China's integrity as defined by the Nine-Power Treaty weakened the general force of his remarks. Negotiations affecting the limited issue of American rights in occupied China, after all, could lead to agreement of such a restricted character as to amount to a virtual underwriting of Japanese aggression in China since 1937. The touchstone in this regard is not so much economic concessions to American nationals as the restoration of a free and independent China.

The published details of Ambassador Grew's conversations with Admiral Nomura, former Japanese Foreign Minister, offered no inkling that the broader issue of China's territorial and administrative integrity was seriously raised by the American government during the negotiations of November-December 1939. Two concessions were made by Japan, so far as the information divulged to the public goes. Certain of the claims for damages to American property were apparently recognized by

[2] See document below, p. 146.

the Japanese government, and restitution has since been made in a number of cases. In December, moreover, the Japanese Foreign Minister informally expressed a willingness to see that the lower Yangtze River would be reopened to international shipping. No specific date for this reopening was set, and it was intimated that certain restrictions (unspecified) would in any case be enforced against foreign shipping between Shanghai and Nanking. On the basis of these trivial concessions, Japan evidently hoped to stave off a "non-treaty situation," if only by the conclusion of a *modus vivendi* on Japanese-American trade relations.

No formal agreement of any kind was reached, and the trade treaty expired on January 26, 1940. At the same time Japan has obtained essentially what its diplomacy sought to achieve, since neither Congress nor the Executive has yet seen fit to place any effective curbs on Japan's access to the American market. State Department policy in this regard was most clearly revealed in the replies given on January 23 to inquiries made by the Japanese Ambassador.[3] The State Department spokesman, Mr. A. A. Berle, Jr., made three points: (1) the possibility of an exchange of notes defining the status of Japanese-American trade relations would be "held open" for consideration during further negotiations at Tokyo; (2) no immediate changes in import duties or tonnage rates on Japanese goods were contemplated; (3) Japanese merchants would be permitted to enter the United States as alien visitors, and could seek visa renewals each year.

Under these conditions, Japan has in fact been able to continue its trading relations with the United States as though the commercial treaty had not expired. The executive branch of the American government has made no effort to use the broad powers which it possesses under existing tariff laws to impose countervailing duties or import restrictions against Japanese goods. A minor extension of the "moral embargo," affecting the construction of petroleum refining plants in Japan (and the Soviet Union) by American firms, was made at the end of January, but no effort to stop the export of petroleum itself to Japan has been instituted.

Nor has any supplementary action been taken by Congress. At the beginning of 1940 two embargo proposals, sponsored by

[3] *New York Times,* January 24, 1940.

Senators Pittman and Schwellenbach, rested in the Senate Foreign Relations Committee. It was generally expected that they would at least be reported out of committee for Senate consideration. The Pittman Resolution authorizes the President to forbid the export of arms and ammunition and certain other specified war materials, such as iron, steel, oil, gasoline and scrap metals, whenever the President finds that any party to the Nine-Power Treaty "is endangering the lives of citizens of the United States or depriving such citizens of their legal rights and privileges." The Schwellenbach Resolution, on the other hand, calls for a mandatory embargo authorizing the President to withhold export of any article or materials (except agricultural products) which "there is reason to believe" will be used in violation of the Nine-Power Treaty. Thus the latter measure will actually prevent Japan from purchasing war materials in the United States, while the Pittman Resolution may or may not do so, depending on whether the President deems it advisable to employ his discretionary authority.

In January and early February Senator Pittman, chairman of the Foreign Relations Committee, indicated through various public statements his expectation that an embargo proposal would be reported to the floor of the Senate. On February 18 the Senate Committee was held to be so evenly divided that a word from Secretary Hull would be decisive; the latter's opposition to Congressional action, however, was tacitly demonstrated by his unwillingness to testify before the Committee.[4] At the next meeting of the Foreign Relations Committee, held on February 21, the embargo resolutions were entirely ignored, despite the fact that Senator Pittman had previously regarded them as the primary items on the calendar.[5] During these weeks it was made clear that the pressure quietly applied by the State Department against Congressional action on the embargo was proving decisive.

Thus, while expiration of the trade treaty has reinforced the threat of economic action against Japan, it has not led to such action. Equal importance attaches to the failure to redefine and restate the broad objectives which American policy is seeking to achieve in the Far East under the new conditions presented by the European war. The *threat* of economic pressure against

[4] *New York Times,* February 18, 1940.

[5] *New York Herald-Tribune,* February 22, 1940.

Japan is a bargaining weapon which can be used for very different ends. At one extreme, it might facilitate the attainment of little more than a compromise agreement at China's expense; at the other—and in this case the threat of action would probably have to be translated into real action—it might lead to a comprehensive Far Eastern settlement on terms equitable to China. The latter course would alone serve as adequate protection for American interests, and at the same time serve to prevent the crystallization of alignments which are tending to spread the European conflict into the Far East. Under present circumstances, the decision on these all important issues is apparently being taken by the American Ambassador in negotiations at Tokyo, but his terms of reference have not been revealed to the American public. There is no public knowledge as to what terms the State Department, or the Ambassador at Tokyo, would consider adequate as a Far Eastern settlement under the new conditions created by the war in Europe.

The American government's obvious unwillingness to impose restrictions on the flow of war supplies to Japan does not reflect American public opinion. A Gallup poll released on Februrary 14, 1940 indicated that an overwhelming majority of the American people favored a ban on the sale of war materials to Japan. Of those polled, 75 per cent expressed themselves in favor of embargo action, and 25 per cent were opposed.[6] This opinion clearly rested on the general knowledge that American war supplies were still being shipped to Japan in undiminished quantity, despite the expiration of the trade treaty.

Far Eastern trade statistics for 1939, published by the Commerce Department on February 21, showed large increases in Japanese purchases during the last four months of the year.[7] Total American exports to Japan aggregated $231 million, compared with $239 million in 1938. American imports from Japan were valued at $161 million, as against $127 million in 1938. The large increase in the value of American imports of Japanese goods was due mainly to the steep rise in the price of Japanese silk which occurred in 1939. Japan's more favorable showing in its 1939 trade balance with countries outside the yen bloc was

[6] *New York Times*, February 14, 1940.

[7] *Trade of the United States with Japan, China, Hongkong and Kwantung, for the year 1939*, press release, Department of Commerce, Washington, D. C., February 21, 1940.

accounted for mainly by the additional $34 million in foreign exchange derived from sales to the United States. In addition to raw silk, the American public during 1939 increased its purchases of Japanese tuna fish, crabmeat, tea, cotton cloth, and chinaware.

Materials essential for war purposes, moreover, have supplied an ever increasing proportion of Japan's purchases in the American market. During the past three years, taking the first eleven months in each case, the ratio of war materials to total American exports to Japan was 58 per cent in 1937, 67 per cent in 1938, and 70 per cent in 1939.[8] Of the war materials supplied to Japan during these years by the United States, approximately 97 per cent was accounted for by petroleum and petroleum products, iron and steel scrap, copper, metal-working machinery, automobiles, parts and accessories, ferro-alloys, iron and steel semimanufactures, aircraft and parts, and lead.

The following table shows a composite balance sheet of Japanese-American trade in 1937-1939, as well as Japan's gold and silver shipments to the United States during this period.

UNITED STATES TRADE WITH JAPAN, 1937–1939

	Exports	*Imports*	*Gold Purchases*	*Silver Purchases*
1937......	$288,558,000	$204,201,000	$246,470,000	$1,273,000
1938......	239,575,000	126,820,000	168,740,000	2,929,000
1939......	231,405,000	161,196,000	165,606,000	4,234,000
Totals...	$769,538,000	$492,217,000	$580,816,000	$8,433,000

These figures afford impressive testimony as to the importance of the American market to Japan. Since 1937 merchandise sold to the United States has supplied Japan with 492 million dollars in foreign exchange, while another 589 million dollars has been derived from the sale of gold and silver to the American Treasury. Japanese imports from the United States during this period, including nearly 50 million dollars worth obtained by Manchoukuo, have aggregated somewhat more than 800 million dollars. Of this latter amount, well over 500 million dollars have consisted of materials essential for war purposes.

Since 1937 the American market has thus been the single most important adjunct of Japan's war machine, enabling the destructive military operations in China to be continued on an increas-

[8] Bulletin No. 17, The Chinese Council for Economic Research, Washington, D. C.

ingly extensive scale. With expiration of the Japanese-American trade treaty on January 26, 1940, it had been widely expected that the economic partnership between the United States and Japan would be severed. Unless a decided change in the attitude of the State Department occurs, however, it now seems possible that Japan will still be able to retain full and unrestricted access to the American market. The twenty million dollar loan to China of March 7, 1940 cannot take the place of effective curbs on Japan's trade with the United States. There is increasing evidence that the failure of the United States to take decisive action in the Far East is stimulating France and Great Britain to seek a separate understanding with Japan. A recent statement by Premier Daladier suggests that France is about to enter into negotiations with Japan relative to formal recognition of Manchoukuo.[9] On February 21, moreover, Senator Gillette applied for information to the State Department regarding "reports that there had been signed or was pending a secret treaty between Great Britain and Japan, looking to mutual recognition of interests in the Far East." At the time State Department experts indicated that "they had heard nothing of such a treaty and that inquiry to the governments concerned had yielded denials that it was in existence or in contemplation."[10]

It is clear, nevertheless, that the possibility of such a move can no longer be safely disregarded. A *fait accompli,* in the form of a definite Anglo-French agreement or treaty with Japan, would confront the United States with a crisis of the first magnitude in the Far East. It would constitute a direct challenge to the historic tenets of American Far Eastern policy, and sweep the Nine-Power Treaty into the discard. Given the existing strength of the American position, as well as the growing economic difficulties faced by Japan, there is no necessity for the United States to defer to an Anglo-French initiative in the Far East. Firm and unequivocal action by the United States at this time would contribute to a Far Eastern settlement that would conserve American interests and do justice to China. Further delay, on whatever pretext it may be based, is likely to play into the hands of Anglo-French policy in the Far East, and lead to an extension of the present limited scope of the hostilities in that region.

[9] *New York Times,* March 1, 1940.
[10] *New York Herald-Tribune,* February 12, 1940.

DOCUMENTS

1. President Roosevelt's Statement Regarding Transport of Munitions to China and Japan on American Ships. September 14, 1937.

"Merchant vessels owned by the Government of the United States will not hereafter, until further notice, be permitted to transport to China or Japan any of the arms, ammunition, or implements of war which were listed in the President's proclamation of May 1, 1937.

Any other merchant vessels, flying the American flag, which attempt to transport any of the listed articles to China or Japan will, until further notice, do so at their own risk.

The question of applying the Neutrality Act remains in *status quo*, the Government policy remaining on a 24 hour basis."

Source: The Department of State, *Press Releases,* September 18, 1937, p. 227.

2. U. S. Note of Protest Against the Bombing of Nanking. September 22, 1937.

"The American Government refers to the statement by the commander in chief of the Japanese Third Fleet which was handed to the American consul general at Shanghai on September 19 announcing the project of the Japanese Naval Air Force, after 12 o'clock noon of September 21, 1937, to resort to bombing and other measures of offense in and around the city of Nanking and warning the officials and nationals of third powers living there 'to take adequate measures for voluntary moving into areas of greater safety.'

"The American Government objects both to such jeopardizing of the lives of its nationals and of noncombatants generally and to the suggestion that its officials and nationals now residing in and around Nanking should withdraw from the areas in which they are lawfully carrying on their legitimate activities.

"Immediately upon being informed of the announcement under reference, the American Government gave instruction to the American Ambassador at Tokyo to express to the Japanese Government this Government's concern; and that instruction was carried out. On the same day the concern of this Government was expressed by the Acting Secretary of State to the Japanese Ambassador in Washington.

"This Government holds the view that any general bombing of an extensive area wherein there resides a large populace engaged in peaceful pursuits is unwarranted and contrary to principles of law and of humanity. Moreover, in the present instance the period allowed for withdrawal is inadequate, and, in view of the wide area over which Japanese bombing operations have prevailed, there can be no assurance that even in areas to which American nationals and noncombatants might withdraw they would be secure.

"Notwithstanding the reiterated assurance that 'the safety of the lives and property of nationals of friendly powers will be taken into full consideration during the projected offensive,' this Government is constrained to observe that experience has shown that, when and where aerial bombing operations are engaged in, no amount of solicitude on the part of the authorities responsible therefor is effective toward insuring the safety of any persons or any property within the area of such operations.

"Reports of bombing operations by Japanese planes at and around Nanking both before and since the issuance of the announcement under reference indicate that these operations almost invariably result in extensive destruction of noncombatant life and nonmilitary establishments.

"In view of the fact that Nanking is the seat of government in China and that there the American Ambassador and other agencies of the American Government carry on their essential functions, the American Government strongly objects to the creation of a situation in consequence of which the American Ambassador and other agencies of this Government are confronted with the alternative of abandoning their establishments or being exposed to grave hazards.

"In the light of the assurances repeatedly given by the Japanese Government that the objectives of Japanese military operations are limited strictly to Chinese military agencies and establishments and that the Japanese Government has no intention of making nonmilitary property and noncombatants the direct objects of attack, and of the Japanese Government's expression of its desire to respect the Embassies, warships, and merchant vessels of the powers at Nanking, the American Government cannot believe that the intimation that the whole Nanking area may be subjected to bombing operations represents the considered intent of the Japanese Government.

"The American Government, therefore, reserving all rights on its own behalf and on behalf of American nationals in respect to damage which might result from Japanese military operations in the Nanking area, expresses the earnest hope that further bombing in and around the city of Nanking will be avoided."

Source: The Department of State, Press Releases, September 22, 1937, pp. 255-6.

3. EXCERPTS FROM PRESIDENT ROOSEVELT'S SPEECH IN CHICAGO. OCTOBER 5, 1937.

". . . If those things come to pass in other parts of the world, let no one imagine that America will escape, that it may expect mercy, that this Western Hemisphere will not be attacked and that it will continue tranquilly and peacefully to carry on the ethics and the arts of civilization. . . .

"If those days are not to come to pass—if we are to have a world in which we can breathe freely and live in amity without fear—the peace-loving nations must make a concerted effort to uphold laws and principles on which alone peace can rest secure.

"The peace-loving nations must make a concerted effort in opposition to those violations of treaties and those ignorings of humane instincts which today are creating a state of international anarchy and instability from which there is no escape through mere isolation or neutrality. . . .

"There is a solidarity and interdependence about the modern world, both technically and morally, which makes it impossible for any nation completely to isolate itself from economic and political upheavals in the rest of the world, especially when such upheavals appear to be spreading and not declining. There can be no stability or peace either within nations or between nations except under laws and moral standards adhered to by all. International anarchy destroys every foundation for peace. It jeopardizes either the immediate or the future security of every nation, large or small. It is, therefore, a matter of vital interest and concern to the people of the United States that the sanctity of international treaties and the maintenance of international morality be restored. . . .

"It is true that the moral consciousness of the world must recognize the importance of removing injustices and well-founded grievances; but at the same time it must be aroused to the cardinal necessity of honoring the sanctity of treaties, or respecting the rights and liberties of others and of putting an end to acts of international aggression.

"It seems to be unfortunately true that the epidemic of world lawlessness is spreading.

"When an epidemic of physical disease starts to spread, the community approves and joins in a quarantine of the patients in order to protect the health of the community against the spread of the disease. . . .

"War is a contagion, whether it be declared or undeclared. It can engulf states and peoples remote from the original scene of hostilities. We are determined to keep out of war, yet we cannot insure ourselves against the disastrous effects of war and the dangers of involvement. We are adopting such measures as will minimize our risk of involvement, but we cannot have complete protection in a world of disorder in which confidence and security have broken down. . . .

"Most important of all, the will for peace on the part of peace-loving nations must express itself to the end that nations that may be tempted to violate their agreements and the rights of others will desist from such a cause. There must be positive endeavors to preserve peace.

"America hates war. America hopes for peace. Therefore, America actively engages in the search for peace."

Source: The Department of State, *Press Releases,* October 9, 1937, pp. 275-9.

4. COMMENT BY THE STATE DEPARTMENT ON THE ACTION TAKEN BY THE LEAGUE ASSEMBLY CONCERNING THE SINO-JAPANESE DISPUTE. OCTOBER 6, 1937.

"The Department of State has been informed by the American Minister to Switzerland of the text of the report adopted by the Advisory Committee of the League of Nations setting forth the Advisory Committee's examination of the facts of the present situation in China and the treaty obligations of Japan. The Minister has further informed the Department that this report was adopted and approved by the Assembly of the League of Nations today, October 6.

Since the beginning of the present controversy in the Far East, the government of the United States has urged upon both the Chinese and the Japanese governments that they refrain from hostilities and has offered to be of assistance in an effort to find some means, acceptable to both parties to the conflict, of composing by pacific methods the situation in the Far East.

The Secretary of State, in statements made public on July 16 and August 23, made clear the position of the government of the United States in regard to international problems and international relationships throughout the world and as applied specifically to the hostilities which are at present unfortunately going on between China and Japan. Among the principles which in the opinion of the government of the United States should govern international relationships, if peace is to be maintained, are abstinence by all nations from the use of force in the pursuit of policy and from interference in the internal affairs of other nations; adjustment of problems in international relations by process of peaceful negotiation and agreement; respect by all nations for the rights of others and observance by all nations of established obligations; and the upholding of the principle of the sanctity of treaties.

On October 5 at Chicago the President elaborated these principles, emphasizing their importance, and in a discussion of the world situation pointed out that there can be no stability or peace either within nations or between nations except under laws and moral standards adhered to by all; that international anarchy destroys every foundation for peace; that it jeopardizes either the immediate or the future security for every nation, large or small; and that it is therefore of vital interest and concern to the people of the United States that respect for treaties and international morality be restored.

In the light of the unfolding developments in the Far East, the government of the United States has been forced to the conclusion that the action of Japan in China is inconsistent with the principles which should govern the relationships between nations and is contrary to the provisions of the Nine-Power Treaty of February 6, 1922, regarding principles and policies to be followed in matters concerning China, and to those of the Kellogg-Briand Pact of August 27, 1928. Thus the conclusions of this Government with respect to the foregoing are in general accord with those of the Assembly of the League of Nations."

Source: The Department of State, *Press Releases,* October 9, 1937, pp. 284-5.

5. Declaration Issued by the Nine-Power Treaty Conference at Brussels. November 24, 1937.

"1. The Nine-Power Treaty is a conspicuous example of numerous international instruments by which the nations of the world enunciate certain principles and accept certain self-denying rules in their conduct with each other, solemnly undertaking to respect the sovereignty of other nations, to refrain from seeking political or economic domination of other nations, and to abstain from interference in their internal affairs.

"2. These international instruments constitute a framework within which international security and international peace are intended to be safeguarded without resort to arms and within which international relationships should subsist on the basis of mutual trust, goodwill, and beneficial trade and financial relations.

"3. It must be recognized that whenever armed force is employed in disregard of these principles the whole structure of international relations based upon the safeguards provided by treaties is disturbed. Nations are then compelled to seek security in ever-increasing armaments. There is created everywhere a feeling of uncertainty and insecurity. The validity of these principles cannot be destroyed by force, their universal applicability cannot be denied, and their indispensability to civilization and progress cannot be gainsaid.

"4. It was in accordance with these principles that this Conference was called in Brussels for the purpose, as set forth in the terms of the invitation issued by the Belgian Government, 'of examining, in accordance with article VII of the Nine-Power Treaty, the situation in the Far East and to consider friendly methods for hastening the end of the regrettable conflict now taking place there.'

"5. Since its opening session on November 3d the Conference has continuously striven to promote conciliation and has endeavored to secure the co-operation of the Japanese Government in the hope of arresting hostilities and bringing about a settlement.

"6. The Conference is convinced that force by itself can provide no just and lasting solution for disputes between nations. It continues to believe that it would be to the immediate and the ultimate interest of both parties to the present dispute to avail themselves of the assistance of others in an effort to bring hostilities to an early end as a necessary preliminary to the achievement of a general and lasting settlement. It further believes that a satisfactory settlement cannot be achieved by direct negotiation between the parties to the conflict alone, and that only by consultation with other powers principally concerned can there be achieved an agreement the terms of which will be just, generally acceptable and likely to endure.

"7. This Conference strongly reaffirms the principles of the Nine-Power Treaty as being among the basic principles which are essential to world peace and orderly progressive development of national and international life.

"8. The Conference believes that a prompt suspension of hostilities in the Far East would be in the best interests not only of China and Japan but of all nations. With each day's continuance of the conflict the loss in lives and property increases and the ultimate solution of the conflict becomes more difficult.

"9. The Conference therefore strongly urges that hostilities be suspended and resort be had to peaceful processes.

"10. The Conference believes that no possible step to bring about by peaceful processes a just settlement of the conflict should be overlooked or omitted.

"11. In order to allow time for participating governments to exchange views and further explore all peaceful methods by which a just settlement of the dispute may be attained consistently with the principles of the Nine-Power Treaty and in conformity with the objectives of that treaty, the Conference deems it advisable temporarily to suspend its sittings. The conflict in the Far East remains, however, a matter of concern to all of the powers assembled at Brussels—by virtue of commitments in the Nine-Power Treaty or of special interest in the Far East—especially to those most immediately and directly affected by conditions and events in the Far East. Those of them that are parties to the Nine-Power Treaty have expressly adopted a policy designed to stabilize conditions in the Far East and, to that end, are bound by the provisions of that treaty, outstanding among which are those of articles I and VII.

"12. The Conference will be called together again whenever its Chairman or any two of its members shall have reported that they consider that its deliberations can be advantageously resumed."

Source: The Conference of Brussels, November 3-24, 1937, pp. 76-7.

6. U. S. Note of Protest Against the Sinking of the U.S.S. Panay. December 13, 1937.

"The Government and people of the United States have been deeply shocked by the facts of the bombardment and sinking of the U. S. S. *Panay* and the sinking or burning of the American steamers *Meiping*, *Meian* and *Meisian* by Japanese aircraft.

"The essential facts are that these American vessels were in the Yangtze River by uncontested and incontestable right; that they were flying the American flag; that they were engaged in their legitimate and appropriate business; that they were at the moment conveying American official and private personnel away from points where danger had developed; that they had several times changed their position, moving upriver, in order to avoid danger; and that they were attacked by Japanese bombing planes. With regard to the attack a responsible Japanese naval officer at Shanghai has informed the Commander-in-Chief of the American Asiatic Fleet that the four vessels were proceeding upriver; that a Japanese plane endeavored to ascertain their nationality, flying at an altitude of three hundred meters, but was unable to distinguish the flags; that three Japanese bombing planes, six Japanese fighting planes, six Japanese bombing planes, and two Japanese bombing planes, in sequence, made attacks which resulted in the damaging of one of the American steamers, and the sinking of the U.S.S. *Panay* and the other two steamers.

"Since the beginning of the present unfortunate hostilities between Japan and China, the Japanese Government and various Japanese authorities at various points have repeatedly assured the Government and authorities of the United States that it is the intention and purpose of the Japanese Government and the Japanese armed forces to respect fully the rights and interests of other powers. On several occasions, however, acts of Japanese armed forces have violated the rights of the United States, have seriously endangered the lives of American nationals, and have destroyed American property. In several instances, the Japanese government has admitted the facts, has expressed regrets, and has given assurance that every precaution will be taken against recurrence of such incidents. In the present case, acts of Japanese armed forces have taken place in complete disregard of American rights, have taken American life, and have destroyed American property both public and private.

"In these circumstances, the Government of the United States requests and expects of the Japanese Government a formally recorded expression of regret, an undertaking to make complete and comprehensive indemnifications; and an assurance that definite and specific steps have been taken which will ensure that hereafter American nationals, interests and property in China will not be subjected to attack by Japanese armed forces or unlawful interference by any Japanese authorities or forces whatsoever."

Source: The Department of State, *Press Releases,* December 18, 1937, pp. 448-9.

7. PRESIDENT ROOSEVELT'S MEMORANDUM TO THE SECRETARY OF STATE. DECEMBER 13, 1937.

"Please tell the Japanese Ambassador when you see him at one o'clock:

1. That the President is deeply shocked and concerned by the news of indiscriminate bombing of American and other non-Chinese vessels on the Yangtse, and that he requests that the Emperor be so advised.

2. That all the facts are being assembled and will shortly be presented to the Japanese Government.

3. That in the meantime it is hoped the Japanese Government will be considering definitely for presentation to this Government:

(a) Full expressions of regret and proffer of full compensation.
(b) Methods guaranteeing against a repetition of any similar attack in the future.

F. D. R."

Source: The Department of State, *Press Releases,* December 18, 1937, p. 447.

8. TO SENATOR WILLIAM H. SMATHERS. DECEMBER 18, 1937.

"My dear Senator Smathers:

I have received your letter of December 13, 1937, in which you inform me that you favor the withdrawal of American ships and citizens from the area affected by the present conflict in the Far East.

The question of the types and degrees of protection which this Government should afford to its citizens abroad presents many difficulties and is one in regard to which opinions may very readily differ. In a situation such as has prevailed in the Far East there have been developed during more than a century certain rights, certain interests, certain obligations and certain practices. In the light of peculiar features inherent in the situation, all of the major powers have developed and employed, with authorization by the Chinese Government, methods for safeguarding the lives and interests and property of their nationals believed to be appropriate to the situation and warranted by the peculiarities thereof. Thus, for instance, there came about and there is still in existence the system of extra-territorial jurisdiction and various of its concomitants. Concurrently, many nationals of this and other countries have, during several generations, gone to China, established themselves there in various occupations and activities, and subjected themselves both to the advantages and to the disadvantages of the conditions prevailing there; and the American Government has, along with other governments, accepted various rights and incurred various obligations. In a situation such as now prevails, many of our nationals cannot suddenly disavow or cut themselves off from the past nor can the American Government suddenly disavow its obligations and responsibilities. The American naval vessels and the small contingents of American land forces which have been maintained in China were placed and have been kept there solely for the purpose of assisting in the maintenance of order and security as affecting the lives, the property and the legitimate activities of American nationals, especially in regard to conditions of local disorder and unauthorized violence. These vessels and troops have never had in any sense any mission of aggression. It has long been the desire and expectation of the American Government that they shall be withdrawn when their appropriate function is no longer called for. We had thought a few months ago that the opportune moment for such a withdrawal was near at hand. The present, however, does not seem an opportune moment for effecting that withdrawal.

Officers of the American Government have repeatedly and earnestly advised American citizens, in face of dangers incident to residence in China, to withdraw and are making every effort to provide safe means whereby they may depart. During the current situation in China the American military and naval forces have rendered important service in protecting the lives of American nationals, in assisting in evacuating Americans from areas of special danger, and in making possible the maintenance of uninterrupted communications with our nationals and our diplomatic and consular establishments in the areas involved.

As of possible interest in this connection there is enclosed a press release issued by the Department on August 23, 1937, outlining the policy on which the Government is proceeding with reference to the situation in the Far East.

I am very grateful for your courtesy in bringing to my attention your views in regard to the situation in the Far East, and I assure you that we welcome at all times thoughtful views and comment on any phase of our foreign relations.

Sincerely yours,

Cordell Hull"

Source: The Department of State, *Press Releases,* December 25, 1937, pp. 495-6.

9. United States Note Accepting Japan's Expression of Regret for the Sinking of the U.S.S. Panay. December 25, 1937.

"The Government of the United States refers to its note of December 14, the Japanese Government's note of December 14 and the Japanese Government's note of December 24 in regard to the attack by Japanese armed forces upon the U.S.S. *Panay* and three American ships.

"In this Government's note of December 14 it was stated that 'the Government of the United States requests and expects of the Japanese Government a formally recorded expression of regret, an undertaking to make complete and comprehensive indemnifications; and an assurance that definite and specific steps have been taken which will ensure that hereafter American nationals, interests and property in China will not be subjected to attack by Japanese armed forces or unlawful interference by any Japanese authorities or forces whatsoever.'

"In regard to the first two items of the request made by the Government of the United States, the Japanese Government's note of December 24 reaffirms statements made in the Japanese Government's note of December 14 which read 'the Japanese Government regret most profoundly that it (the present incident) has caused damages to the United States' man-of-war and ships and casualties among those on board, and desire to present hereby sincere apologies. The Japanese Government will make indemnifications for all the losses and will deal appropriately with those responsible for the incident.' In regard to the third item of the request made by the Government of the United States, the Japanese Government's note of December 24 recites certain definite and specific steps which the Japanese Government has taken to ensure, in words of that note, 'against infringement of, or unwarranted interference with, the rights and interests of the United States and other third powers' and states that 'the Japanese Government is thus endeavoring to preclude absolutely all possibility of the recurrence of incidents of a similar character.'

"The Government of the United States observed with satisfaction the promptness with which the Japanese Government in its note of December 14 admitted responsibility, expressed regret, and offered amends.

"The Government of the United States regards the Japanese Government's account, as set forth in the Japanese Government's note of December 24, of action taken by it as responsive to the request made by the Government of the United States in this Government's note of December 14.

"With regard to the facts of the origins, causes and circumstances of the incident, the Japanese Government indicates in its note of December 24 the conclusion at which the Japanese Government, as a result of its investigation, has arrived. With regard to these same matters, the Government of the United States relies on the report of findings of the Court of Inquiry of the United States Navy, a copy of which has been communicated officially to the Japanese Government.

"It is the earnest hope of the Government of the United States that the steps which the Japanese Government has taken will prove effective toward preventing any further attacks upon or unlawful interference by Japanese authorities or forces with American nationals, interests or property in China."

Source: The Department of State, *Press Releases,* December 25, 1937, pp. 498-9.

10. SECRETARY HULL'S LETTER TRANSMITTING INFORMATION REQUESTED IN SENATE RESOLUTION 210. JANUARY 8, 1938.

Department of State
Washington, D. C.
January 8, 1938

"The Vice President
United States Senate
Sir:

On January 6, I received a copy attested by the Secretary of the Senate of Senate Resolution No. 210 of January 5, 1938, which reads as follows:

'Resolved, That the Secretary of State is requested to transmit to the Senate at the earliest practicable time the following information, based upon the latest available statistics: (1) The approximate number of American nationals residing in the Republic of China on or about August 9, 1936, the number temporarily in China on said date, and the number now residing therein; (2) if not inconsistent with the public interest, the approximate number of officers and enlisted personnel of our Army, Navy, and Marine Corps now stationed in said Republic; and (3) the approximate amount of American capital invested in said Republic and the names and addresses of the principal investors.'

In reply:

1. The request for figures giving the approximate number of American nationals residing in the Republic of China on or about August 9, 1936, the number temporarily in China on said date, and the number now residing therein, can be answered only by the use of and the making of certain estimates. The figures available to the Department are approximate figures as of the dates January 1, 1936, January 1, 1937, and November 6, 1937.

(a) On the basis of figures relating to January 1, 1936, and the figures relating to January 1, 1937, it is the Department's belief that the number of American residents in China as of August 9, 1936, would approximate 10,350.

(b) For the number of American nationals temporarily in China on or about August 9, 1936, there are no figures available. However, there were issued or renewed during the year 1936 for travel in the Far East American passports to the number of 10,636, and it is to be presumed that a considerable number of the persons who received these passport services visited China (or, if residing there, were there or returned thereto) during that year.

(c) With regard to the number of American nationals now residing in the Republic of China, the information available to the Department indicates that in July 1937 at the beginning of the present Sino-Japanese hostilities there were in China approximately 10,500 American nationals; that of this number some 4,600 were evacuated up to November 6; and that there now are in China approximately 6,000 American nationals.

2. With regard to the approximate number of officers and enlisted personnel of our Army, Navy, and Marine Corps stationed in the Republic of China, the United States now has armed forces ashore at three points in China:

At Peiping (U. S. Marines).........	528
At Tientsin (U. S. Army)..........	814
At Shanghai (U. S. Marines).......	2,555

Of the force of U. S. Marines at Shanghai approximately 1,500 represent reinforcements and relief sent to that port in August 1937 for temporary duty as a result of and in order to cope with problems occasioned by the present emergency situation in the way of protecting American nationals. Approximately 100 of this reinforcement have already been withdrawn.

With regard to the approximate number of officers and enlisted personnel of our Navy stationed in Chinese waters, I am informed by the Navy Department that at this time the total personnel on all United States naval vessels now in Chinese waters is 129 officers and 1,671 men, including marines on ships. This personnel is on 13 United States naval vessels, which constitute a part of the United States Asiatic Fleet, based on Manila. The United States Asiatic Fleet comprises 44 vessels, which, with the exception of the flagship, the U.S.S. *Augusta,* a heavy cruiser, are ships of the lighter categories—destroyers, submarines and gunboats, with certain auxiliary vessels. Of the 44 vessels of the Asiatic Fleet, only 13 are now in Chinese waters and of this 13 only 9, consisting for the most part of small, river gunboats, are on duty exclusively in Chinese waters. These 9 gunboats have a total personnel of 69 officers and 896 men.

3. With regard to the approximate amount of American capital invested in the Republic of China and the names and addresses of the principal investors, the most authoritative information available to the Department of State as to American investments in China is that contained in the statement which the Secretary of Commerce sent to Senator Gerald P. Nye under date January 4, 1938, the text of which is published in the *Congressional Record* of January 5, pages 63, 64. For convenience of reference there is quoted the first paragraph of the statement furnished by the Secretary of Commerce, reading as follows:

'The latest official figures of American investments abroad on a by-country basis are those published in the Balance of International Payments of the United States in 1933, pages 53 to 62. Insofar as China is concerned, the total remains practically the same as in 1933—$132,000,000. To this total, for some purposes, may be added (1) approximately $40,000,000 of Chinese obligations that have been in default since the World War; (2) from twenty-five to thirty million dollars to cover the properties of American citizens permanently residing in China; and (3) about $40,000,000 of properties of American missionary and charitable organizations.'

With regard to the names and addresses of the principal American investors, the Department maintains no complete lists of individual American investors in China and is not authoritatively informed as to the amount of the investments of individual firms, societies, or organizations. Professor Charles F. Remer's book entitled *Foreign Investments in China* (the Macmillan Company, New York, 1933)—which is referred to in the statement of the Secretary of Commerce mentioned above—contains statements that American "business investments" include the investments of 352 different firms, of men in the various professions, and of clubs and similar organizations; that the property of American missions and philanthropic societies, nine Catholic societies or orders, and ten educational, medical, and philanthropic institutions.

It may be considered of interest as a part of the background of general policy to give additional information and comment as follows:

With regard to the U. S. Marine detachment at Peiping and the U. S. Army detachment at Tientsin, the American Government maintains these small detachments—and several other interested governments maintain similar detachments—pursuant to the provisions of the so-called Boxer Protocol of 1901 which was concluded between China and the representatives of the interested governments, including the American Minister to China. The purpose of maintaining these troops is to contribute to the protection of American nationals (including the diplomatic personnel) and, in case of emergency calling for evacuation, making available an armed escort.

With regard to the U. S. Marine detachment at Shanghai, the Government of the United States has since 1927—as have various other governments—maintained in the International Settlement at that port a small detachment of armed forces for the purpose of assisting in protecting the large number of American citizens residing in that area from the dangers incident to serious disorders possibly beyond the control of the local authorities.

With regard to the United States naval vessels in Chinese waters, the Government of the United States has—as have other similarly interested governments—maintained gunboats in Chinese waters since the 1840's primarily for the purpose of contributing to the protection of American citizens. The authority for stationing naval vessels in Chinese waters is found in the Sino-American Treaty of 1858 and in provisions of somewhat similar treaties between China and other foreign powers which provisions inure to the benefit of the United States through most-favored-nation treatment.

American armed forces in China are there for the protection of American nationals primarily against mobs or other uncontrollable elements. They have no mission of aggression. It has been the desire and the intention of the American Government to remove these forces when performance of their function of protection is no longer called for, and such remains its desire and expectation. Developments in China during the years immediately preceding the outbreak of the present hostilities between China and Japan afforded the Government of the United States reasonable expectation that the armed forces of this country might soon be withdrawn from China in an orderly way and to the advantage of this and other countries. The normal trend of events however, was interrupted when fighting broke out and spread to various parts of China.

During the current situation in China—as in various previous situations of emergency—the American armed forces in China have rendered important service in protecting the lives of American nationals, in assisting in evacuating Americans from areas of special danger, and in making possible the maintenance of uninterrupted communications with and for our nationals and our diplomatic and consular establishments in the areas involved.

Confronted by the present emergency situation in the Far East, which is attended by extraordinary hazards to everyone in the affected areas, this Government has endeavored to accord to American nationals in that region appropriate and practicable protection, as the Government of the United States always has done in similar situations in all parts of the world. From approximately 1825 until the outbreak of the Spanish-American War, the United States maintained a squadron of naval vessels in the Mediterranean, primarily for the purpose of according protection in the broadest possible sense to American citizens. Subsequent to the World War, the United States maintained a squadron of naval vessels in European waters for the same general purpose. This squadron was gradually withdrawn. In July, 1936, when civil war developed in Spain there happened to be a number of United States naval vessels cruising in European waters. Because of the hazard to the lives of American nationals in Spain and with a view to facilitating withdrawal of American citizens from that country and rendering needed protection, three of the United States naval vessels then in European waters were sent to Spanish ports; also, a United States Coast Guard cutter which was then in European waters. The United States now maintains three naval vessels in proximity to Spanish waters for the purpose indicated above. Thus what the Government of the United States is doing in China is entirely consistent with long-established policy and practice of the United States and the well-recognized duty of the Government to afford protection to American nationals.

The interest and concern of the United States in the Far Eastern situation, in the European situation, and in situations on this continent are not measured by the number of American citizens residing in a particular country at a particular moment nor by the amount of investment of American citizens there nor by the volume of trade. There is a broader and much more fundamental interest—which is that orderly processes in international relationships be maintained. Referring expressly to the situation in the Far East, an area which contains approximately half the population of the world, the United States is deeply interested in supporting by peaceful means influences contributory to preservation and encouragement of orderly processes. This interest far transcends in importance the value of American trade with China or American investments in China; it transcends even the question of safeguarding the immediate welfare of American citizens in China.

In connection with the problem of affording appropriate protection to Americans in China, there must be kept in mind the fact that we have nationals residing in practically every country of the world and that every year some 200,000 of our citizens go abroad; that these include large numbers of students, teachers, religious leaders, laborers, executives and merchants, men, women, and children; that the number of Americans proceeding abroad for business purposes is not greater than, is probably less than, the number who go abroad for educational, cultural and philanthropic purposes; and that a policy of abandoning American nationals in any one part of the world would have inevitable and serious repercussions adverse to the legitimate rights of Americans and the legitimate interests of this country in other parts, in most parts, of the world.

In emergency situations such as that which now prevails in the Far East, the Government endeavors to pursue in regard to the question of affording appropriate protection a course based upon calm reason. We endeavor to afford those measures of protection which are called for by and are in accord with the realities of the situation. Since the beginning of the present Chinese-Japanese conflict, this government and its officers in China have repeatedly and earnestly advised American citizens, in face of dangers incident to situations of danger, to withdraw, and in the present situation we are making every effort to provide safe means whereby they may depart. When situations of acute danger develop or seem likely to develop at particular points, our officers redouble their efforts to effect the safe withdrawal of American citizens from those points. When the situation at particular points becomes more tranquil and less likely to present serious hazard to the lives of American citizens, the course is followed of withdrawing armed forces which may have been sent to those points.

In the present situation in the Far East, the Government of the United States is affording appropriate protection and assistance to American nationals, as this Government always has done. The American Government is also upholding principles, as it has always done. It has asked and is asking that the rights of the United States and the rights of our people be respected, and at the same time it has sought and is seeking to avoid involvement of this country in the disputes of other countries.

The principles which the Government of the United States is following in its international relationships are set forth in the statement which I made on July 16, 1937. A copy of this statement and a copy of a further statement which I made on August 23 are enclosed for convenience of reference. We are directing our whole thought and effort toward making effective the policies, especially the policy of peace, in which this country believes and to which it is committed.

I have the honor (etc.)

Cordell Hull"

Source: The Department of State, *Press Releases,* January 15, 1938, pp. 100-5.

11. U. S. Note of Protest Against Violation of American Rights in the Lower Yangtze Valley. January 17, 1938.

"I am instructed by my Government to bring to Your Excellency's attention reports and complaints from American residents that in the course of recent military operations at Nanking, Hangchow, and other places the Japanese armed forces have repeatedly entered American property illegally and removed goods and employees and committed other acts of depredation against American property which has almost invariably been marked by American flags and by notices in English, Chinese and Japanese issued by the American authorities and setting forth the American character of the property concerned. According to these reports not only have Japanese soldiers manifested a complete disregard for these notices but they have also in numerous instances torn down, burned and otherwise mutilated American flags. I am directed to impress upon Your Excellency the seriousness with which my Government regards such acts and to convey its most emphatic protest against them. My Government finds it impossible to reconcile the flagrant disregard of American rights shown by Japanese troops as above described with the assurances contained in Your Excellency's note of December 24,

1937, that 'rigid orders have been issued to the military, naval and Foreign Office authorities to pay . . . greater attention than hitherto to observance of the instructions that have been repeatedly given against infringement of, or unwarranted interference with, the rights and interests of the United States and other third powers.'

"In view of the fact that a number of these acts are reported as having occurred subsequent to the receipt of the aforementioned assurances of the Imperial Japanese Government and inasmuch as this disregard of American rights is reported as still continuing, the American Government is constrained to observe that the steps which the Japanese Government have so far taken seem inadequate to ensure that hereafter American nationals, interests and property in China shall not be subjected to attack by Japanese armed forces or unlawful interference by any Japanese authorities or forces whatsoever. My Government must, therefore, request that the Imperial Japanese Government reenforce the instructions which have already been issued in such a way as will serve effectively to prevent the repetition of such outrages."

Source: The Department of State, *Press Releases,* January 29, 1938, pp. 177-8.

12. Substance of American Note Relative to Japanese Warning to Foreign Nationals to Withdraw from Designated Areas in China. Issued by State Department on February 25, 1938.

"There rests upon American officials and other American nationals in China no obligation whatsoever to take precautionary measures requested on behalf of the contending forces toward safeguarding American lives and interests. Precautionary measures have voluntarily been advised by this government and its officials, and they have been voluntarily undertaken insofar as possible, and such measures will continue voluntarily to be taken. Nevertheless, irrespective of whether American nationals take or do not take such precautionary measures as are suggested, the obligation remains on the Japanese military authorities to exert the utmost precaution to the end that American nationals and property shall not be injured by their military operations. Whether requests of the Japanese military authorities have or have not been complied with, if American nationals or property are injured in consequence of the operations of Japanese armed forces, the United States Government will be compelled to attribute to the government controlling the armed forces responsibility for the damage."

Source: *New York Times,* February 26, 1938.

13. U. S. Note to Japan Presenting Claims for Damages Incurred in the Sinking of the Panay. March 21, 1938.

"Reference is made to the exchanges of communications between my Government and the Government of Japan regarding the attack upon the U.S.S. *Panay* and American merchant vessels on December 12, 1937, by Japanese armed forces and to the assurances contained in your Government's note dated December 14, 1937, and reaffirmed in its note of December 24, 1937, that the Japanese Government would make 'indemnifications for all the losses sustained.'

"I am instructed by my Government to state that it finds (1) that the amount of the property losses sustained is $1,945,670.01, and (2) that the amount of the indemnification which should be paid in the death and personal injury cases is $268,337.35. Therefore the total amount which my Government is prepared to accept is $2,214,007.36.

"These figures have been arrived at after careful consideration and represent only the actual property losses and a conservative estimate of the damages resulting from deaths and personal injuries. The amount includes no item of punitive damages."

Source: The Department of State, *Press Releases,* March 26, 1938, p. 410.

14. U. S. Note, Exchanged with Other Signatories of the London Naval Treaty of 1936, Giving Notice of Intention to Escalate under Article 25 of That Treaty. March 31, 1938.

"With reference to Article 25 of the Naval Treaty signed in London on March 25, 1936, I have the honor to notify Your Excellency, in accordance with paragraph (2) of that Article, that the Government of the United States of America finds it necessary to exercise the right of escalation reserved in paragraph (1) and of effecting a departure from the limitations and restrictions of the Treaty.

"The proposed departure relates to the upper limits of capital ships of sub-category (a) and to the calibre of guns which may be mounted on capital ships of sub-category (a).

"The above action is motivated by the fact that upon receipt of reports to the effect that Japan is constructing or has authorized the construction of capital ships of a tonnage and armament not in conformity with the limitations and restrictions of the Treaty, the Government of the United States addressed an inquiry to the Japanese Government and the Japanese Government did not choose to furnish information with regard to its present naval construction or its plans for future construction."

Source: The Department of State, *Press Releases,* April 2, 1938, p. 437.

15. U. S. NOTE REGARDING STATUS OF AMERICAN PROPERTY IN CHINA OCCUPIED BY JAPANESE FORCES. MAY 31, 1938.

"The problem of enabling American citizens in China to re-enter and repossess their properties, from which they have been excluded by the Japanese military and of which the Japanese military have been and in some cases still are in occupation, is giving the Government of the United States increasing concern.

"An illustrative case is that of the property of the University of Shanghai, a large and valuable plant located at Shanghai in the Yangtzepoo district. This university has been engaged for many years in educational work and is jointly owned by the Northern and Southern Baptist Missionary Societies. The premises of the university have been under continuous occupation by Japanese military and naval units since shortly after the outbreak of hostilities at Shanghai in August 1937. It is understood that the premises have been used by the Japanese for quartering troops and for military offices, and a portion of the campus for stationing airplanes and supplementing the runway for airplanes on the adjacent golf course which has been converted by the Japanese into a military flying field. During the period of Japanese occupancy several buildings have been damaged and the majority looted. Japanese occupation of the property has continued for a period of nine months, notwithstanding the fact that hostilities in this locality long ago ceased. Repeated written and oral representations made by the American Embassy at Tokyo to the Japanese Government and by the American Consul General at Shanghai to the Japanese authorities there have not so far resulted in bringing about restoration of the premises to the rightful owners. Recently, representatives of the Baptist missionary societies have stressed, on behalf of the six million Baptists in the United States, the urgent need for the return to their possession of this important missionary educational property.

"In various places in the lower Yangtze Valley American business men and missionaries have been prevented by the Japanese authorities from returning to their places of business and mission stations and are denied even casual access to their properties. The American Consul General at Shanghai has made applications for passes in behalf of several American firms with important interests in that area, in order to permit the representatives and employees of the firms to resume business there, but such applications have repeatedly been refused by the Japanese authorities on the ground that peace and order have not been sufficiently restored. This has been the case even when the applications were for visits for the purpose of taking steps to prevent further deterioration of their properties, including stocks and equipment, during their enforced absence. Many Japanese merchants and their families are known to be in the localities to which these Americans seek to return.

"American missionaries also have been prevented from returning to their stations in the lower Yangtze Valley. Certain mission properties in this region which were formerly under occupation by Japanese troops are now reported to have been vacated as a result of Japanese troop transfers, and the missionary societies concerned feel it highly important that their representatives reoccupy and preserve such properties. In view of the fact that Japanese civilians are freely permitted to go into and reside in such areas—as, for example, at Nanking where some eight hundred Japanese nationals, including a substantial number of women and children, are reported to be in residence—it is difficult to perceive any warrant for the continued placing by the Japanese authorities of obstacles in the way of return by Americans who have legitimate reason for proceeding to the areas in question.

"My Government is confident that the Japanese Government cannot but concede that the infringement of and interference with American rights in China by the Japanese authorities involved in the situation to which attention is herein brought are contrary to the repeated assurances of the Japanese Government that the American rights will be respected; that the Japanese Government will take immediate steps, in keeping with such assurances, to cause the return to their rightful owners of the premises of the University of Shanghai and other American property under the occupation of Japanese armed forces; and that the Japanese Government will issue instructions to have removed the obstacles interposed by the Japanese authorities in China against return by American nationals to places such as those mentioned in the areas under Japanese military occupation."

Source: The Department of State, *Press Releases,* June 4, 1938, pp. 635-7.

16. Warning Addressed by Commerce Department to American Exporters Regarding Payment for Goods Shipped to Japan. June 1938.

"In view of all the factors involved, it appears advisable that exporters should have a confirmed irrevocable letter of credit in their hands before accepting orders for shipments to Japan.

"The procurement of exchange permits in Japan is becoming increasingly difficult and is a matter of growing concern to Japanese importers. It is understood that certain Japanese firms have recently contracted with American exporters on the basis of payment before arrival of the goods in Japan. It would appear, however, that Japanese importers have no means of foretelling in advance whether or not their applications for exchange permits will be granted. Private Japanese importers are obviously not in a position to bind the Ministry of Finance in this matter. Although it is understood that certain contracts of this nature have been successfully consummated in the past, such instances afford no assurance as to the future.

"In view of the increasing severity with which the exchange restrictions in Japan are being enforced, it is believed that a confirmation irrevocable letter of credit offers the American exporter the most satisfactory assurance that the Japanese importer has fully complied with the regulations and that payment will be duly forthcoming."

Source: *The Christian Science Monitor,* June 22, 1938.

17. TEXT OF PROTOCOL TO LONDON NAVAL TREATY OF 1936, AND ACCOMPANYING STATEMENT BY THE AMERICAN GOVERNMENT. JUNE 30, 1938.

"Following the refusal of Japan to furnish information with regard to its naval construction, or its plans for future construction, the powers parties to the London Naval Treaty of 1936—that is, the United States, Great Britain, and France—mutually reached the decision to depart from the limits of the treaty in the battleship category and, on April 1, exchanged notes announcing their intention to escalate.

"Under the terms of the treaty, the next step following the formal announcement of intention to escalate is consultation over a period of three months to determine whether new limits can be fixed and if so what these new limits will be. Accordingly, the representatives of the three powers met at London on April 12 and at intervals thereafter in order to explore the possibilities of limitation.

"All three powers, in this consultation, took the ground that, in view of all the circumstances, there must be a departure from the limits of the treaty. The United States, wishing to maintain in effect naval limitation insofar as possible, informed the other signatory powers of its willingness to accept a new limitation of 45,000 tons on the size and 16 inches in the armament of capital ships. When it is decided to build larger capital ships, these limits are, from a technical point of view, believed most nearly to correspond with the naval defense needs of the United States.

"The protocol signed today at London by the signatories to the London treaty of 1936 gives formal approval to the fixing of the new limitation to the tonnage of capital ships. . . . The text is as follows:

'Whereas by Article Four (1) of the Treaty for the Limitation of Naval Armaments signed in London on 25th March, 1936, it is provided that no capital ship shall exceed 35,000 tons (35,560 metric tons) standard displacement;

'And whereas by reason of Article Four (2) of the said Treaty the maximum calibre of gun carried by capital ships is 16 inches (406 mm.);

'And whereas on the 31st March, 1938, His Majesty's Government in the United Kingdom of Great Britain and Northern Ireland and the Government of the United States of America gave notice under paragraph (2) of Article 25 of the said Treaty of their decision to exercise the right provided for in paragraph (1) of the said Article to depart from the limitations and restrictions of the Treaty in regard to the upper limits of capital ships of sub-category (a);

'And whereas consultations have taken place as provided in paragraph (3) of Article 25, with a view to reaching agreement in order to reduce to a minimum the extent of the departures from the limitations and restrictions of the Treaty;

'The undersigned, duly authorized by their respective governments have agreed as follows:

'One. As from this day's date the figure of 35,000 tons (35,560 metric tons) in Article Four (1) of the said Treaty shall be replaced by the figure of 45,000 tons (45,720 metric tons).

'Two. The figure of 16 inches (406 mm.) in Article Four (2) remains unaltered.

'Three. The present protocol, of which the French and English texts shall both be equally authentic, shall come into force on this day's date.

'In faith whereof the undersigned have signed the present protocol.

'Done in London the 30th day of June, 1938.'

"The British Government has today addressed a note to the Government of the United States stating that the two capital ships provided for in the current year's estimates will not exceed 40,000 tons (40,640 metric tons). The note also states that should it at any time be found necessary to construct capital ships of a higher tonnage than 40,000 tons (40,640 metric tons) notification of such intention would be made in the ordinary way to the other interested powers in accordance with the provisions of the London Naval Treaty of 1936."

Source: The Department of State, *Press Releases,* July 2, 1938, pp. 10-11.

18. U. S. NOTE OF PROTEST AGAINST JAPANESE ATTACK ON COMMERCIAL PLANE. AUGUST 26, 1938.

"Excellency:

"Acting under instructions, I have the honor on behalf of my Government to protest to Your Excellency against the unwarranted attack on August 24, 1938 near Macao, by Japanese airplanes upon a commercial airplane operated by the China National Aviation Corporation resulting in a total destruction of the commercial airplane, the loss of the lives of a number of non-combatant passengers, and the endangering of the life of the American pilot.

"This attack upon the plane has aroused public feeling in the United States.

"I am directed to point out to Your Excellency, with reference to the attack in question, that not only was the life of an American national directly imperilled but loss was also occasioned to American property interests as the Pan American Airways has a very substantial interest in the China National Aviation Corporation.

"I am directed to invite the special attention of Your Excellency to the following points in the account of Pilot Wood: The China National Aviation Corporation plane was pursued by Japanese planes which started machine gunning; after the China National Aviation Corporation plane had successfully landed it was followed down by Japanese pursuit planes which continued to machine gun it until it had sunk; and when Pilot Wood started swimming across the river he was followed by one of the Japanese planes which continued to machine gun him.

"My Government desires to express its emphatic objection to the jeopardizing in this way of the lives of American as well as other non-combatant occupants of unarmed planes engaged in clearly recognized and established commercial services over a regularly scheduled air route.

"I avail myself (etc.),

Joseph C. Grew"

Source: The Department of State, *Press Releases,* August 27, 1938, pp. 146-7.

19. U. S. Note to Japan Regarding Japanese Violation of American Rights in China. October 6, 1938.

"The Government of the United States has had frequent occasion to make representations to Your Excellency's Government in regard to action taken and policies carried out in China under Japanese authority to which the Government of the United States takes exception as being, in its opinion, in contravention of the principle and the conditions of equality of opportunity or the 'Open Door' in China. In response to these representations, and in other connections, both public and private, the Japanese Government has given categorical assurances that equality of opportunity or the Open Door in China will be maintained. The Government of the United States is constrained to observe, however, that notwithstanding the assurances of the Japanese Government in this regard violations by Japanese agencies of American rights and interests have persisted.

"As having, by way of illustration, a bearing upon the situation to which the Government of the United States desires to invite the attention of the Japanese Government, it is recalled that at the time of the Japanese occupation of Manchuria the Japanese Government gave assurances that the Open Door in Manchuria would be maintained. However, the principal economic activities in that area have been taken over by special companies which are controlled by Japanese nationals and which are established under special charters according them a preferred or exclusive position. A large part of American enterprise which formerly operated in Manchuria has been forced to withdraw from that territory as a result of the preferences in force there. The arrangements between Japan and the regime now functioning in Manchuria allow the free movement of goods and funds between Manchuria and Japan while restricting rigidly the movement of goods and funds between Manchuria and countries other than Japan.

"This channeling of the movement of goods is effected primarily by means of exchange control exercised under the authority of regulations issued under an enabling law which provide expressly that for the purposes of the law Japan shall not be considered a foreign country nor the Japanese yen a foreign currency. In the opinion of my Government equality of opportunity or the Open Door has virtually ceased to exist in Manchuria notwithstanding the assurances of the Japanese Government that it would be maintained in that area.

"The Government of the United States is now apprehensive lest there develop in other areas of China which have been occupied by Japanese military forces since the beginning of the present hostilities a situation similar in its adverse effect upon the competitive position of American business to that which now exists in Manchuria.

"On April 12, 1938, I had occasion to invite the attention of Your Excellency's predecessor to reports which had reached the Government of the United States indicating that discrimination in favor of Japanese trade with North China was likely to be effected by means of exchange control and to ask for assurances that the Japanese Government would not support or countenance financial measures discriminatory against American interests. Although the Minister for Foreign Affairs stated then that the Japanese Government would continue to support the principle of equal opportunity or the Open Door in China, no specific reply has yet been made by the Japanese Government on the subject of these representations.

"The Government of the United States now learns that the Japanese authorities at Tsingtao have in effect established an exchange control, that they are exercising a discretionary authority to prohibit exports unless export bills are sold to the Yokohama Specie Bank, and that the Bank refuses to purchase export bills except at an arbitrary rate far lower than the open market rate prevailing at Tientsin and Shanghai. A somewhat similar situation apparently prevails at Chefoo. Furthermore, reports continue to reach the American Government that a comprehensive system of exchange control will soon be established throughout North China. Control of foreign exchange transactions gives control of trade and commercial enterprise, and the exercise, either directly or indirectly, by the Japanese authorities of control of exchange in North China would place those authorities in position to thwart equality of opportunity or free competition between Japan and the United States in that area. In such a situation, imports from and exports to the United States, as well as the choice of dealers in North China, would be entirely subjected to the dispensation of the Japanese authorities. Notwithstanding the short time that the exchange control has been enforced in Tsingtao, two cases of discrimination have already been brought to the attention of the Government of the United States. In one instance an American dealer in a staple commodity has been unable to export to the United States because Japanese authorities there have insisted that his export bills be sold to a Japanese bank at a rate so far below the current rate of exchange of the Chinese currency in the open market that such transactions would involve a loss rather than a profit; but a Japanese competitor recently completed a large shipment invoiced at a price in United States dollars which was equivalent to the local market price calculated at the current open market rate. In the other instance, an American firm was prevented from purchasing tobacco in Shantung unless it should purchase so-called Federal Reserve Notes or yen currency with foreign exchange and at an arbitrary and low rate of exchange, conditions not imposed upon the company's Japanese or Chinese competitors.

"The Government of the United States has already pointed out to the Japanese Government that alterations of the Chinese customs tariff by the regimes functioning in those portions of China occupied by Japanese armed forces and for which the Japanese Government has formally assured its support are arbitrary and illegal assumptions of authority for which the Japanese Government has an inescapable responsibility. It is hardly necessary to add that there can be no equality of opportunity or Open Door in China so long as the ultimate authority to regulate, tax, or prohibit trade is exercised, whether directly or indirectly, by the authorities of one 'foreign' power in furtherance of the interests of that power.

"It would appear to be self-evident that a fundamental prerequisite of a condition of equality of opportunity or Open Door in China is the absence in the economic life of that country of preferences or monopolistic rights operating directly or indirectly in favor of any foreign country or its nationals. On July 4, I spoke to General Ugaki of the desire of the American Government that there would be avoided such restrictions and obstacles to American trade and other enterprises as might result from the setting up of special companies and monopolies in China. The Minister was so good as to state that the Open Door in China would be maintained and that the Government of the United States might rest assured that the Japanese Government would fully respect the principle of equal opportunity.

"Notwithstanding these assurances, the provisional regime in Peiping announced on July 30th the inauguration as of the following day of the China Telephone and Telegraph Company, the reported purpose of this organization being to control and to have exclusive operation of telephone and telegraph communications in North China. There was organized in Shanghai on July 31st the Central China Telecommunications Company, and the Special Service Section of the Japanese Army has informed foreign cable and telegraph companies that the new company proposes to control all the telecommunications in central China. According to a semi-official Japanese press report there was organized at Shanghai on July 28 the Shanghai Inland Navigation Steamship Company, to be controlled by Japanese, the reported object of which is to control water transportation in the Shanghai delta area. According to information which has reached my Government, a Japanese company has been organized to take over and operate the wharves at Tsingtao which have hitherto been publicly owned and operated. Should such a development occur, all shipping of whatever nationality would become dependent upon a Japanese agency for allotments of space and stevedoring facilities. The wool trade in North China is now reported to be a Japanese monopoly and a tobacco monopoly in that area is reported to be in process of formation. Moreover, according to numerous reports which have been reaching my Government, the Japanese Government is proceeding with the organization of two special promotion companies which it has chartered and which it will control with the object of investing in, unifying, and regulating the administration of certain large sectors of economic enterprise in China.

"The developments of which I have made mention are illustrative of the apparent trend of Japanese policy in China and indicate clearly that the Japanese authorities are seeking to establish in areas which have come under Japanese military occupation general preferences for, and superiority of, Japanese interests, an inevitable effect of which will be to frustrate the practical application of the principle of the Open Door and deprive American nationals of equal opportunity.

"I desire also to call Your Excellency's attention to the fact that unwarranted restrictions placed by the Japanese military authorities upon American nationals in China—notwithstanding the existence of American treaty rights in China and the repeated assurances of the Japanese Government that steps had been taken which would insure that American nationals, interests, and properties would not be subject to unlawful interference by Japanese authorities—further subject American interests to continuing serious inconvenience and hardship. Reference is made especially to the restrictions placed by the Japanese military upon American nationals who desire to reenter and reoccupy properties from which they have been driven by hostilities and of which the Japanese military have been or still are in occupation. Mention may also be made of the Japanese censorship of and interference with American mail and telegrams at Shanghai, and of restrictions upon freedom of trade, residence and travel by Americans, including the use of railways, shipping, and other facilities. While Japanese merchant vessels are carrying Japanese merchandise between Shanghai and Nanking, those vessels decline to carry merchandise of other countries, and American and other non-Japanese shipping is excluded from the lower Yangtze on the grounds of military necessity. Applications by American nationals for passes which would allow them to return to certain areas in the lower Yangtze Valley have been denied by the Japanese authorities on the ground that peace and order have not been sufficiently restored, although many Japanese merchants and their families are known to be in those areas.

"American nationals and their interests have suffered serious losses in the Far East arising from causes directly attributable to the present conflict between Japan and China, and even under the most favorable conditions an early rehabilitation of American enterprise in China and of American trade with China cannot be expected. The American Government, therefore, finds it all the more difficult to reconcile itself to a situation in which American nationals must contend with continuing unwarranted interference with their rights at the hands of the Japanese authorities in China and with Japanese actions and policies which operate to deprive American trade and enterprise of equality of opportunity in China. It is also pertinent to mention that in Japan, too, American trade and other interests are undergoing severe hardships as a result of the industrial, trade, exchange and other controls which the Japanese Government has imposed incident to its military operations in China.

"While American interests in the Far East have been thus treated at the hands of the Japanese authorities, the Government of the United States has not sought either in its own territory or in the territory of third countries to establish or influence the establishment of embargoes, import prohibitions, exchange controls, preferential restrictions, monopolies or special companies designed to eliminate or having the effect of eliminating Japanese trade and enterprise. In its treatment of Japanese nationals and their trade and enterprise, the American Government has been guided not only by the letter and spirit of the Japanese-American Commercial Treaty of 1911 but by those fundamental principles of international law and order which have formed the basis of its policy in regard to all peoples and their interests; and Japanese commerce and enterprise have continued to enjoy in the United States equality of opportunity.

"Your Excellency cannot fail to recognize the existence of a great and growing disparity between the treatment accorded American nationals and their trade and enterprise by Japanese authorities in China and Japan and the treatment accorded Japanese nationals and their trade and enterprise by the Government of the United States in areas within its jurisdiction.

"In the light of the situation herein reviewed, the Government of the United States asks that the Japanese Government implement its assurances already given with regard to the maintenance of the Open Door and to non-interference with American rights by taking prompt and effective measures to cause:

(1) The discontinuance of discriminatory exchange control and of other measures imposed in areas in China under Japanese control which operate directly or indirectly to discriminate against American trade and enterprise;

(2) The discontinuance of any monopoly or of any preference which would deprive American nationals of the right of undertaking any legitimate trade or industry in China, or of any arrangement which might purport to establish in favor of Japanese interests any general superiority of rights with regard to commercial or economic development in any region of China; and

(3) The discontinuance of interference by Japanese authorities in China with American property and other rights including such forms of interference as censorship of American mail and telegrams, and restrictions upon residence and travel by Americans and upon American trade and shipping.

"The Government of the United States believes that in the interest of relations between the United States and Japan an early reply would be helpful."

Source: The Department of State, *Press Releases,* October 29, 1938, pp. 283-6.

20. STATEMENT OF PRESIDENT ROOSEVELT REGARDING THE REPORT OF THE JOINT PREPARATORY COMMITTEE ON PHILIPPINE AFFAIRS. NOVEMBER 29, 1938.

"The report of the Joint Preparatory Committee on Philippine Affairs, which is being released to the public today in Washington and Manila, has the approval of the President of the United States as the basis of Congressional consideration for the purpose of correcting the imperfections and inequalities of the Independence Act of March 24, 1934, against which the Filipino people have complained, and for the purpose of making more certain and definite the future commercial relationships between the United States and the Philippines after Philippine independence is attained.

"The accomplishment of these two objectives is important and urgent. Changes must be made in existing law before November 1940 if the disruption of several Philippine industries is to be avoided. In addition, it is desirable that at an early date some definite indication should be given by the legislative and executive branches of the United States Government as to the future commercial policy of the United States toward an independent Philippines so that the official and commercial representatives of the two countries can make such adjustments as may be required because of the relinquishment of United States sovereignty over the Philippines in 1946."

Source: The Department of State, *Press Releases,* December 3, 1938, pp. 383-4.

21. U. S. Note to Japan Regarding Violation of American Rights in China. December 31, 1938.

"The Government of the United States has received and has given full consideration to the reply of the Japanese Government of November 18 to this Government's note of October 6 on the subject of American rights and interests in China.

"In the light of facts and experience the Government of the United States is impelled to reaffirm its previously expressed opinion that imposition of restrictions upon the movements and activities of American nationals who are engaged in philanthropic, educational and commercial endeavors in China has placed and will, if continued, increasingly place Japanese interests in a preferred position and is, therefore, unquestionably discriminatory, in its effect, against legitimate American interests. Further, with reference to such matters as exchange control, compulsory currency circulation, tariff revision, and monopolistic promotion in certain areas of China, the plans and practices of the Japanese authorities imply an assumption on the part of those authorities that the Japanese Government or the regimes established and maintained in China by Japanese armed forces are entitled to act in China in a capacity such as flows from rights of sovereignty and, further, in so acting to disregard and even to declare non-existent or abrogated the established rights and interests of other countries, including the United States.

"The Government of the United States expresses its conviction that the restrictions and measures under reference not only are unjust and unwarranted but are counter to the provisions of several binding international agreements, voluntarily entered into, to which both Japan and the United States, and in some cases other countries, are parties.

"In the concluding portion of its note under reference, the Japanese Government states that it is firmly convinced that 'in the face of the new situation, fast developing in East Asia, any attempt to apply to the conditions of today and tomorrow inapplicable ideas and principles of the past neither would contribute toward the establishment of a real peace in East Asia nor solve the immediate issues,' and that 'as long as these points are understood, Japan has not the slightest inclination to oppose the participation of the United States and other powers in the great work of reconstructing East Asia along all lines of industry and trade.'

"The Government of the United States in its note of October 6 requested, in view of the oft-reiterated assurances proffered by the

Government of Japan of its intention to observe the principle of equality of opportunity in its relations with China, and in view of Japan's treaty obligations so to do, that the Government of Japan abide by these obligations and carry out these assurances in practice. The Japanese Government in its reply appears to affirm that it is its intention to make its observance of that principle conditional upon an understanding by the American Government and by other governments of a 'new situation' and a 'new order' in the Far East as envisaged and fostered by Japanese authorities.

"Treaties which bear upon the situation in the Far East have within them provisions relating to a number of subjects. In the making of those treaties, there was a process among the parties to them of give and take. Toward making possible the carrying out of some of their provisions, others among their provisions were formulated and agreed upon; toward gaining for itself the advantage of security in regard to certain matters, each of the parties committed itself to pledges of self-denial in regard to certain other matters. The various provisions agreed upon may be said to have constituted collectively an arrangement for safeguarding, for the benefit of all, the correlated principles on the one hand of national integrity and on the other hand of equality of economic opportunity. Experience has shown that impairment of the former of these principles is followed almost invariably by disregard of the latter. Whenever any government begins to exercise political authority in areas beyond the limits of its lawful jurisdiction there develops inevitably a situation in which the nationals of that government demand and are accorded, at the hands of their government, preferred treatment, whereupon equality of opportunity ceases to exist and discriminatory practices, productive of friction, prevail.

"The admonition that enjoyment by the nationals of the United States of non-discriminatory treatment in China—a general and well-established right—is henceforth to be contingent upon an admission by the Government of the United States of the validity of the conception of Japanese authorities of a 'new situation' and a 'new order' in East Asia, is, in the opinion of this Government, highly paradoxical.

"This country's adherence to and its advocacy of the principle of equality of opportunity do not flow solely from a desire to obtain the commercial benefits which naturally result from the carrying out of that principle. They flow from a firm conviction that observance of that principle leads to economic and political stability, which are conducive both to the internal well-being of nations and to mutually beneficial and peaceful relationships between and among nations; from a firm conviction that failure to observe that principle breeds international friction and ill-will, with consequences injurious to all countries, including in particular those countries which fail to observe it; and from an equally firm conviction that observance of that principle promotes the opening of trade channels thereby making available the markets, the raw materials and the manufactured products of the community of nations on a mutually and reciprocally beneficial basis.

"The principle of equality of economic opportunity is, moreover, one to which over a long period and on many occasions the Japanese Government has given definite approval. It is one to the observance of which the Japanese Government has committed itself in various international agreements and understandings. It is one upon observance of which by other nations the Japanese Government has of its own accord and upon its own initiative frequently insisted. It is one to which the Japanese Government has repeatedly during recent months declared itself committed.

"The people and the Government of the United States could not assent to the establishment, at the instance of and for the special purposes of any third country, of a regime which would arbitrarily deprive them of the long-established rights of equal opportunity and fair treatment which are legally and justly theirs along with those of other nations.

"Fundamental principles, such as the principle of equality of opportunity, which have long been regarded as inherently wise and just, which have been widely adopted and adhered to, and which are general in their application, are not subject to nullification by a unilateral affirmation.

"With regard to the implication in the Japanese Government's note that the 'conditions of today and tomorrow' in the Far East call for a revision of the ideas and principles of the past, this Government desires to recall to the Japanese Government its position on the subject of revision of agreements.

"This Government had occasion in the course of a communication delivered to the Japanese Government on April 29, 1934, to express its opinion that 'treaties can lawfully be modified or be terminated, but only by processes prescribed or recognized or agreed upon by the parties to them.'

"In the same communication this Government also said, 'In the opinion of the American people and the American Government no nation can, without the assent of the other nations concerned, rightfully endeavor to make conclusive its will in situations where there are involved the rights, the obligations and the legitimate interests of other sovereign states.'

"In an official and public statement on July 16, 1937, the Secretary of State of the United States declared that this Government advocates 'adjustment of problems in international relations by processes of peaceful negotiation and agreement.'

"At various times during recent decades various powers, among which have been Japan and the United States, have had occasion to communicate and to confer with regard to situations and problems in the Far East. In the conducting of correspondence and of conferences relating to these matters, the parties involved have invariably taken into consideration past and present facts and they have not failed to perceive the possibility and the desirability of changes in the situation. In the making of treaties they have drawn up and have agreed upon provisions intended to facilitate advantageous developments and at the same time to obviate and avert the arising of friction between and among the various powers which, having interests in the region or regions under reference, were and would be concerned.

"In the light of these facts, and with reference especially to the purpose and the character of the treaty provisions from time to time solemnly agreed upon for the very definite purposes indicated, the Government of the United States deprecates the fact that one of the parties to these agreements has chosen to embark—as indicated both by action of its agents and by official statements of its authorities—upon a course directed toward the arbitrary creation by that power by methods of its own selection, regardless of treaty pledges and the established rights of other powers concerned, of a 'new order' in the Far East. Whatever may be the changes which have taken place in the situation in the Far East and whatever may be the situation now, these matters are of no less interest and concern to the American Government than have been the situations which have prevailed there in the past, and such changes as may henceforth take place there, changes which may enter into the producing of a 'new situation' and a 'new order,' are and will be of like concern to this Government. This Government is well aware that the situation has changed. This Government is also well aware that many of the changes have been brought about by action of Japan. This Government does not admit, however, that there is need or warrant for any one power to take upon itself to prescribe what shall be the terms and conditions of a 'new order' in areas not under its sovereignty and to constitute itself the repository of authority and the agent of destiny in regard thereto.

"It is known to all the world that various of the parties to treaties concluded for the purpose of regulating contacts in the Far East and avoiding friction therein and therefrom—which treaties contained, for those purposes, various restrictive provisions—have from time to time and by processes of negotiation and agreement contributed, in the light of changed situations, toward the removal of restrictions and toward the bringing about of further developments which would warrant, in the light of further changes in the situation, further removals of restrictions. By such methods and processes, early restrictions upon the tariff autonomy of all countries in the Far East were removed. By such methods and processes, the rights of extraterritorial jurisdiction once enjoyed by occidental countries in relations with countries in the Far East have been given up in relations with all of those countries except China; and in the years immediately preceding and including the year 1931, countries which still possess those rights in China, including the United States, were actively engaged in negotiations—far advanced—looking toward surrender of those rights. All discerning and impartial observers have realized that the United States and other of the 'treaty powers' have not during recent decades clung tenaciously to their so-called 'special' rights and privileges in countries of the Far East but on the contrary have steadily encouraged the development in those countries of institutions and practices in the presence of which such rights and privileges may safely and readily be given up; and all observers have seen those rights and privileges gradually being surrendered voluntarily, through agreement, by the powers which have possessed them. On one point only has the Government of the United States, along with several other governments, insisted: namely, that new situations must have developed to a point warranting the removal of 'special' safeguarding restrictions and that the removals be effected by orderly processes.

"The Government of the United States has at all times regarded agreements as susceptible of alteration, but it has always insisted that alterations can rightfully be made only by orderly processes of negotiation and agreement among the parties thereto.

"The Japanese Government has upon numerous occasions expressed itself as holding similar views.

"The United States has in its international relations rights and obligations which derive from international law and rights and obligations which rest upon treaty provisions. Of those which rest on treaty provisions, its rights and obligations in and with regard to China rest in part upon provisions in treaties between the United States and China, and in part upon provisions in treaties between the United States and several other powers, including both China and Japan. These treaties were concluded in good faith for the purpose of safeguarding and promoting the interest not of one only but of all of their signatories. The people and the Government of the United States cannot assent to the abrogation of any of this country's rights or obligations by the arbitrary action of agents or authorities of any other country.

"The Government of the United States has, however, always been prepared, and is now, to give due and ample consideration to any proposals based on justice and reason which envisage the resolving of problems in a manner duly considerate of the rights and obligations of all parties directly concerned by processes of free negotiation and new commitment by and among all of the parties concerned. There has been and there continues to be opportunity for the Japanese Government to put forward such proposals. This Government has been and it continues to be willing to discuss such proposals, if and when put forward, with representatives of the other powers, including Japan and China, whose rights and interests are involved, at whatever time and in whatever place may be commonly agreed upon.

"Meanwhile, this Government reserves all rights of the United States as they exist and does not give assent to any impairment of any of those rights."

Source: The Department of State, *Press Releases,* December 31, 1938, pp. 490-3.

22. Excerpt from President Roosevelt's Message to Congress. January 4, 1939.

"We have learned that God-fearing democracies of the world which observe the sanctity of treaties and good faith in their dealings with other nations cannot be safely indifferent to international lawlessness anywhere. They cannot forever let pass, without effective protest, acts of aggression against sister nations—acts which automatically undermine all of us.

"Obviously they must proceed along practical, peaceful lines. But the mere fact that we rightly decline to intervene with arms to prevent acts of aggression does not mean that we must act as if there were no aggression at all. Words may be futile, but war is not the only means of commanding a decent respect for the opinions of mankind. There are many methods short of war, but stronger and more effective than mere words, of bringing home to aggressor governments the aggregate sentiments of our own people.

"At the very least, we can and should avoid any action, or any lack of action, which will encourage, assist or build up an aggressor. We have learned that when we deliberately try to legislate neutrality, our neutrality laws may operate unevenly and unfairly—may actually give aid to an aggressor and deny it to the victim. The instinct of self-preservation should warn us that we ought not to let that happen any more."

Source: *New York Times,* January 5, 1939.

23. THE AIDE-MEMOIRE OF MAY 17, 1939 DEALING WITH THE INTERNATIONAL SETTLEMENT AT SHANGHAI.

"Reference is made to the *aide-mémoire* which the Japanese Vice Minister for Foreign Affairs handed to the American Ambassador at Tokyo on May 3 in regard to the question of revision of the Land Regulations of the International Settlement and to the question of modifying and improving the administrative machinery of the International Settlement.

"The *aide-mémoire* contains reference to the date on which the Land Regulations now in force in the International Settlement at Shanghai became effective and contains the affirmation that the existing administrative structure is in many respects ill adapted for dealing with factors in the situation which has been steadily evolving during the past seventy and more years and which has undergone a radical change in more recent times.

"The Government of the United States would be ready, as it has been in the past, to become a party to friendly and orderly negotiations properly instituted and conducted regarding any needed revision in the Land Regulations of the International Settlement at Shanghai. The Government of the United States is constrained to point out, however, that conditions in the Shanghai area are, from its viewpoint, so far from normal at the present time that there is totally lacking a basis for the discussion looking toward an orderly settlement of the complicated problems involved which would be reasonably fair to all concerned.

"With reference to the question of the Chinese courts which function in the International Settlement, it may be pointed out that those courts were established and their status fixed under a multilateral agreement to which the United States Government was a party and that the observations made in regard to possible revision of the Land Regulations apply also to the question of these courts.

"With regard to the system of voting in force in the municipal elections and public meetings of the International Settlement, it may be observed that under the Land Regulations there is no discrimination amongst the various foreign rate payers, the minimum requirement for voting qualification being the payment of municipal rates on the basis of an assessed rental of 500 taels (approximately seven hundred dollars Chinese currency) per annum. Under this system the Japanese community enjoys a large and increasingly important vote, a vote in fact far greater in proportion to the total vote than the proportion which the general municipal rates and land taxes paid by the Japanese community bear to the total of the municipal rates and land taxes paid in the International Settlement. Japanese nationals are represented on the Municipal Council and are employed in the various departments of the Municipal Government.

"With regard to the question of modifying and improving the administrative machinery of the International Settlement, the Government of the United States believes that the Japanese Government will recognize that those concerned with the administration of the International Settlement have, throughout the Settlement's history, effected many adjustments to meet changing conditions and the Government of the United States is confident that the authorities of the Settlement will continue to make every effort to adjust the administrative machinery of the Settlement and the practices thereof to meet fair and reasonable desires on the part of Japan and Japanese interests.

"With reference to the statement in the Japanese *aide-mémoire* in regard to the need for closer co-operation between the Settlement authorities and the regimes which exist in the lower Yangtze Valley with Japanese military support, it may be observed that, in the absence of the duly constituted and recognized Government of that area, the Settlement authorities have made and are making every effort to deal with the realities of the very difficult situation confronting them, and the Government of the United States feels that those authorities are entitled to expect every consideration from Japanese civil and military agencies. It is pertinent to point out in this connection that since the earliest days of the International Settlement it has necessarily been the policy of the Settlement authorities, during periods of disturbance in the surrounding areas, to avoid involvement in controversial matters arising from causes beyond the Settlement boundaries. This aloofness is inherent in the very international character of the Settlement. And logically flowing therefrom is the premise that no one power having interests in the Settlement, however extensive they may be, should take advantage of developments which have their origin elsewhere to prejudice the international character of the Settlement.

"The Government of the United States has been impressed with the efficiency and energy with which the Settlement authorities have, notwithstanding the extreme bitterness and tense atmosphere prevailing at Shanghai, kept disorder and lawlessness to a minimum within that part of the International Settlement which is under their effective control.

"The Government of the United States refers again to the efforts which the authorities of the International Settlement have been making and are continuing to make to perform their normal functions, efforts which have recently been seriously handicapped and rendered more difficult by lawless activities in areas contiguous to the International Settlement and by refusal on the part of the Japanese military forces to return the Settlement area lying north of Soochow Creek to the effective control of the authorities of the International Settlement.

"The Government of the United States urges upon the Japanese Government the consideration that a smooth working of the administrative machinery of the Settlement would be promoted by a frank recognition on the part of the Japanese Government of the excellent work which has been and is being done by the Settlement authorities and by the prompt restoration to those authorities of complete control over the Settlement area extending north of Soochow Creek.

"In conclusion, the Government of the United States observes that the great cosmopolitan center of Shanghai has been developed by the nationals of many countries, to the mutual advantage of all. In this development the International Settlement has played a very important part and any question affecting the welfare or status of the Settlement is of inevitable concern to many countries, including the United States. With regard to the revision of the Land Regulations, the Government of the United States is, as indicated above, of the opinion that this is a question which should await the development of more stable conditions. But with regard to administrative practice in the Settlement, many adjustments have been made to meet the requirements of changing conditions, and the Government of the United States is confident that the Settlement authorities are prepared to continue their best efforts toward meeting any reasonable requests for further adjustments."

Source: The Department of State, *Press Releases,* May 20, 1939, pp. 421-3.

24. Press Conference Statement of Secretary Hull Regarding the Tientsin Dispute. June 19, 1939.

"This Government is not concerned in the original incident at Tientsin relating to the requested delivery of the four accused Chinese. It is concerned, however, with the nature and significance of subsequent developments, in their broader aspects, coupled with other past and present acts and utterances in other parts of China. This Government, therefore, is observing with special interest all related developments in China as they occur from day to day. I have nothing further to add today."

Source: The Department of State, *Press Releases,* June 24, 1939, p. 541.

25. U. S. Notice to Japan of Termination of the Treaty of 1911. July 26, 1939.

"During recent years the Government of the United States has been examining the treaties of commerce and navigation in force between the United States and foreign countries with a view to determining what changes may need to be made toward better serving the purposes for which such treaties are concluded. In the course of this survey, the Government of the United States has come to the conclusion that the Treaty of Commerce and Navigation between the United States and Japan which was signed at Washington on February 21, 1911, contains provisions which need new consideration. Toward preparing the way for such consideration and with a view to better safeguarding and promoting American interests as new developments may require, the Government of the United States, acting in accordance with the procedure prescribed in Article XVII of the treaty under reference, gives notice hereby of its desire that this treaty be terminated, and, having thus given notice, will expect the treaty, together with its accompanying protocol, to expire six months from this date."

Source: The Department of State, *Bulletin,* July 29, 1939, p. 81.

26. Extract from an Address Delivered by the American Ambassador Before the America-Japan Society, Tokyo, Japan. October 19, 1939.

". . . I turn now to some of the thoughts of the American Government and of the American people with regard to the situation in East Asia in general and to our relations with Japan in particular. It is trite to say—but all too often the fact is overlooked—that in our democratic system the policies and measures of our Government reflect, and inevitably must reflect, public opinion. If therefore in any given case or situation we search for the underlying causation of American policy, or of any specific measure or measures of our Government. In this connection I have not for a moment lost sight of the force of public opinion in Japan.

"Obviously American public opinion is frequently divided; seldom is it unanimous. In the face of a divided public opinion, the Government must choose between acting according to its judgment as to what will best serve the interests of the country and withholding action altogether. But when public opinion is unanimous, or nearly unanimous, then governmental policy and action must and will reflect the opinion and wishes of the people as a whole. For the American Government is the servant of the American people. American public opinion with regard to recent and current developments in the Far East is today very nearly unanimous, and that opinion is based not on mere hearsay or on propaganda but on facts.

"Among the conditions existing in the United States which impress me more and more vividly each time I return to my country are: First, the freedom which prevails in public discussion; and second, the demand for knowledge of facts and the intelligent appraisal of those facts by men and women in every walk of life. Especially is this true today in regard to foreign affairs. It is not alone the Government official or the student or the businessman or the manufacturer or the financier who keeps his finger on the pulse of our foreign relations. This interest—and it is a keen, living interest—extends to the masses—the factory hand, the servant in the house, the taxi driver in the street. In the past few months at home I have been immensely impressed by the intelligent grasp by people in every quarter of what is going on in every corner of the world. I have been drawn into discussion of foreign affairs not only by men and women in important and influential positions but by travelers in the smoking compartment of railroad trains, by the stewards in airplanes, by the men and women behind the counters in the stores and shops, by the attendants at gasoline stations, by the drivers of taxis who were taking me to some destination. And what impressed me most was that these people not only knew what was going on abroad but had formed their own individual opinions of those events and of what the United States should or should not do about it. Those people, mostly, are widely read. My chiropodist, when I entered his room, was reading an important book on Japan, and we discussed that book throughout the session. A farmer in the small New England village where we live lent me another recent book on Japan. In the many talks which I had with many, many people, I received the distinct impression that those people are sufficiently well-informed and sufficiently wide awake to distinguish between fact and propaganda. I do not suppose that any country in the world is better served today, by press and radio, with accurate foreign information than is the United States. In every country there are of course certain elements of the press inclined toward sensationalism, but the vast majority of the American people today read and demand the despatches and comments of correspondents and commentators of proved reliability for accurate reporting. Propaganda not based on fact, or distorting fact, is anathema to the average American. And the senseless propaganda with which foreign countries sometimes try to influence public opinion in our country does the countries of its origin and the interests of those countries far more harm than good. The average American, knowing the facts, sees through it and will have none of it.

"Here, then, is the stuff of which public opinion in the United States is built. It is only through such individual contacts as I enjoyed this summer that one comes to appreciate the tremendous force of public opinion in our country and to realize its fabric and its power. When such opinion tends toward unanimity in any given issue, it is a force which the Government cannot possibly overlook and will not fail to reflect in its policies and actions.

"What am I to say to you today? Would it be the act of a friend of Japan, a friend of the members of this society, would it be in the interests of Japanese-American relations which this society steadily labors to build up and improve, if I were to misstate the truth or try to obscure it by painting an inaccurate picture of my observations at home? If an ambassador is in effect an interpreter, mustn't he interpret correctly on the basis of facts known to him? And on returning from a long stay in America, would it not insult your intelligence if I were to talk of trivialities? I suppose that there is not a person here who does not know that American public opinion strongly resents some of the things that Japan's armed forces are doing in China today, including actions against American rights and legitimate interests in China. On that subject public opinion in the United States is unanimous. And, mind you, I know whereof I speak, from personal talks with a very large number of people in diverse walks of life throughout our country, constituting a reliable cross-section of the American public.

"If we then accept as a regrettable fact this state of American public opinion, and we must accept it as a fact, then isn't it from every point of view, especially from the point of view of statesmanship, reasonable and logical that we should in all frankness examine the basic causes of that state of public opinion? I know those causes in general and in detail. It would be harmful to overlook them. I earnestly believe that those causes must be removed and that by their removal only constructive good can come to both our Nations. The attainment of such mutually constructive good, needless to say, is and has been and always will be the fundamental purpose of my ambassadorship to Japan.

"Before I left for America last May a Japanese friend of mine begged me to tell my friends in America the situation in Japanese-American relations as he conceived it. It ran somewhat as follows:

"American rights and interests in China are suffering some minor and unimportant inconveniences in China as a result of Japanese military operations; the Japanese military take every possible precaution to avoid inconvenience to American interests; reports published in the United States in regard to damage to American interests by the Japanese in China are intentionally exaggerated in order to inflame the American people against Japan; in large measure those activities of the Japanese to which Americans object are the result of differences in customs, differences in language, and a legalistic attitude which has been adopted by the United States; in the near future the situation in the occupied areas of China will be so improved that the United States will no longer have any cause of complaint. That was the point of view of my Japanese friend.

"Alas, the truth is far otherwise. The facts, as they exist, are accurately known by the American Government. They are likewise known by the American people, and in the interests of the future relations between Japan and the United States those facts must be faced. Only through consideration of those facts can the present attitude of the American Government and people toward Japan be understood; only through consideration of those facts, and through constructive steps to alter those facts, can Japanese-American relations be improved. Those relations *must* be improved.

"Having said all this I do not propose today to deal in detail with the causations which have brought about that feeling in my country. This is not the occasion to enter any 'bill of particulars.' Those facts, those difficulties between our Nations, are matters for consideration by the two Governments; indeed, some of them are matters which I have been discussing with the Japanese Government during the past two years, and I shall continue to approach these matters. But I believe that the broad outline of those facts and difficulties are known to you. Some of those difficulties are serious.

"Now many of you who are listening to me may well be thinking: 'There are two sides to every picture; we in Japan also have our public opinion to consider.' Granted. In America, as I have already said, I did my best to show various angles of the Japanese point of view. But here in Japan I shall try to show the American point of view. Without careful consideration of both points of view we can get nowhere in building up good relations. I wish you could realize how intensely I wish for that most desirable end and how deeply I desire, by pure objectivity, to contribute to a successful outcome. Let me therefore try to remove a few utterly fallacious conceptions of the American attitude as I think they exist in Japan today.

One of these fallacies is that the American approach to affairs in East Asia is bound by a purely 'legalistic' attitude, a conception which widely prevails in this country today. What is meant by a 'legalistic' attitude? If we mean respect for treaties, official commitments, international law, yes; that respect is and always will be one of the cardinal principles of American policy. But the very term 'a legalistic attitude' as it has often been used in my hearing in Japan, seems to imply a position where one cannot see the woods for the trees, where one's vision of higher and broader concepts is stultified. Let me therefore touch briefly on a few of the cardinal principles of American policy and objectives, moulded to meet the requirements of modern life, which, it is true, are fundamentally based upon but which seem to me far to transcend any purely 'legalistic' approach to world affairs.

"The American people aspire to relations of peace with every country and between all countries. We have no monopoly on this desire for peace, but we have a very definite conviction that the sort of peace which, throughout history, has been merely an interlude between wars is not an environment in which world civilization can be stably developed or, perhaps, can even be preserved. We believe that international peace is dependent on what our Secretary of State has characterized as 'orderly processes' in international dealing.

"The American people desire to respect the sovereign rights of other people and to have their own sovereign rights equally respected. We have found by experience that the successful approach to the resolving of international disputes lies not so much in merely abstaining from the use of force as in abstaining from any thought of the use, immediately or eventually, of the methods of force. Let cynics look about them and contemplate the consequences of resort to menacing demands as a process in the conduct of international relations. Is it being purely 'legalistic' to put to wise and practical use the finer instincts common to all mankind?

"The American people believe that the day is past when wars can be confined in their effects to the combatant nations. When national economies were based upon agriculture and handcraft, nations were to a large extent self-sufficient; they lived primarily on the things which they themselves grew or produced. That is not the case today. Nations are now increasingly dependent on others both for commodities which they do not produce themselves and for the disposal of the things which they produce in excess. The highly complex system of exchange of goods has been evolved by reason of each nation's being able to extract from the ground or to manufacture certain commodities more efficiently or economically than others. Each contributes to the common good the fruits of its handiwork and the bounties of nature. It is this system of exchange which has not only raised the standard of living everywhere but has made it possible for two or even three persons to live in comfort under a simple self-contained economy. Not only the benefits of our advanced civilization but the very existence of most of us depends on maintaining in equilibrium a delicately balanced and complex world economy. Wars are not only destructive of the wealth, both human and material, of combatants, but they disturb the fine adjustments of world economy. Conflict between nations is therefore a matter of concern to all the other nations. Is there then any stultification through 'legalistic' concepts when we practice ourselves and urge upon others the resolving of international disputes by orderly processes, even if it were only in the interests of world economy? How, except on the basis of law and order, can these various concepts in international dealing be secured?

"The American people believe in equality of commercial opportunity. There is probably no nation which has not at one time or other invoked it. Even Japan, where American insistence on the 'open door' is cited as the supreme manifestation of what is characterized as a 'legalistic' American attitude—even Japan, I say—has insisted upon and has received the benefits of the "open door" in areas other than China, where, we are told, the principle is inapplicable except in a truncated and emasculated form. That highly complicated system of world economy of which I have just spoken is postulated upon the ability of nations to buy and sell where they please under conditions of free competition—conditions which cannot exist in areas where preemptive rights are claimed and asserted on behalf of nationals of one particular country.

"I need hardly say that the thoughts which I have just expressed are of universal applicability.

"Another common fallacy which I am constrained to mention is the charge that the American Government and people do not understand 'the new order in East Asia.' Forgive me if I very respectfully take issue with that conception. The American Government and people understand what is meant by the 'new order in East Asia' precisely as clearly as it is understood in Japan. The 'new order in East Asia' has been officially defined in Japan as an order of security, stability, and progress. The American Government and people earnestly desire security, stability, and progress not only for themselves but for all other nations in every quarter of the world. But the new order in East Asia has appeared to include, among other things, depriving Americans of their long-established rights in China, and to this the American people are opposed.

"There's the story. It is probable that many of you are not aware of the increasing extent to which the people of the United States resent the methods which the Japanese armed forces are employing in China today and what appear to be their objectives. In saying this, I do not wish for one moment to imply that the American people have forgotten the long-time friendship which has existed between the people of my country and the people of Japan. But the American people have been profoundly shocked over the widespread use of bombing in China, not only on grounds of humanity but also on grounds of the direct menace to American lives and property accompanied by the loss of American life and the crippling of American citizens; they regard with growing seriousness the violation of and interference with American rights by the Japanese armed forces in China in disregard of treaties and agreements entered into by the United States and Japan and treaties and agreements entered into by several nations, including Japan. The American people know that those treaties and agreements were entered into voluntarily by Japan and that the provisions of those treaties and agreements constituted a practical arrangement for safeguarding—for the benefit of all—the correlated principles of national sovereignty and of equality of economic opportunity. The principle of equality of economic opportunity is one to which over a long period and on many occasions Japan has frequently insisted. Not only are the American people perturbed over their being arbitrarily deprived of long-established rights, including those of equal opportunity and fair treatment, but they feel that the present trend in the Far East if continued will be destructive of the hopes which they sincerely cherish of the development of an orderly world. American rights and interests in China are being impaired or destroyed by the policies and actions of the Japanese authorities in China. American property is being damaged or destroyed; American nationals are being endangered and subjected to indignities. If I felt in a position to set forth all the facts in detail today, you would, without any question, appreciate the soundness and full justification of the American attitude. Perhaps you will also understand why I wish today to exercise restraint.

"In short, the American people, from all the thoroughly reliable evidence that comes to them, have good reason to believe that an effort is being made to establish control, in Japan's own interest, of large areas on the continent of Asia and to impose upon those areas a system of closed economy. It is this thought, added to the effect of the bombings, the indignities, the manifold interference with American rights, that accounts for the attitude of the American people toward Japan today. For my part I will say this. It is my belief of the American Government and people, that the many things injurious to the United States which have been done and are being done by Japanese agencies are wholly needless. We believe that real security and stability in the Far East could be attained without running counter to any American rights whatsoever.

"Mr. Chairman, Ladies and Gentlemen: I have tried to give an accurate interpretation of American public opinion, most carefully studied and analyzed by me while at home. The traditional friendship between our two Nations is far too precious a thing to be either inadvertently or deliberately impaired. It seems to me logical that from every point of view—economic, financial, commercial, in the interests of business, travel, science, culture, and sentiment—Japan and the United States forever should be mutually considerate friends. In the family of nations, as between and among brothers, there arise inevitable controversies, but again and again the United States has demonstrated its practical sympathy and desire to be helpful toward Japan in difficult times and moments, its admiration of Japan's achievements, its earnest desire for mutually helpful relations.

"Please do not misconstrue or misinterpret the attitude which has prompted me to speak in the utmost frankness today. I am moved first of all by love of my own country and my devotion to its interest; but I am also moved by very deep affection for Japan and by sincere conviction that the real interests, the fundamental and abiding interests of both countries, call for harmony of thought and action in our relationships. Those who know my sentiments for Japan, developed in happy contacts during the seven years in which I have lived here among you, will realize, I am sure, that my words and my actions are those of a true friend.

"One Japanese newspaper queried, on my return from America, whether I had concealed in my bosom a dagger or a dove. Let me answer that query. I have nothing concealed in my bosom except the desire to work with all my mind, with all my heart, and with all my strength for Japanese-American friendship.

"Today I have stated certain facts, straight-forwardly and objectively. But I am also making a plea for sympathetic understanding in the interests of the old, enduring friendship between our two great Nations. In a world of chaos I plead for stability, now and in the long future, in a relationship which, *if it can be preserved,* can bring only good to Japan and the United States of America."

Source: *The Department of State Bulletin,* Vol. I, No. 20, November 11, 1939, pp. 509-516.

INDEX